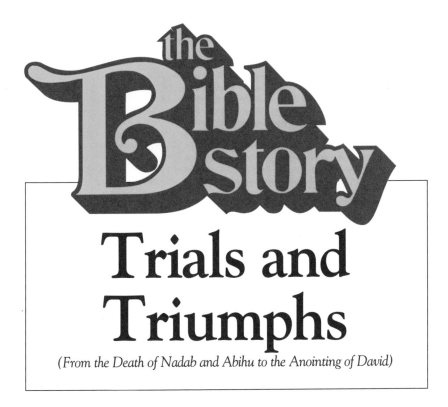

the Bible story

Trials and Triumphs

(From the Death of Nadab and Abihu to the Anointing of David)

VOLUME THREE

the Bible story

Trials and Triumphs ❖ Volume Three

Arthur S. Maxwell
Author of Uncle Arthur's *Bedtime Stories*

When Arthur S. Maxwell wrote *The Bible Story*, he used the King James Version of the Bible, closely following its narrative. This edition continues that tradition and draws from other translations using language that today's children readily understand.

NEWLY REVISED AND ILLUSTRATED

More than 400 stories in 10 Volumes Covering the Entire Bible From Genesis to Revelation

REVIEW AND HERALD® PUBLISHING ASSOCIATION
HAGERSTOWN, MD 21740

This book was
Revised by Cheryl Holloway
Edited by Eugene Lincoln
Cover art by Harry Anderson

PRINTED IN U.S.A.

R&H Cataloging Service
Maxwell, Arthur Stanley,
1896-1970
    The Bible story.
    1. Bible stories.   I. Title.
II. Holloway, Cheryl Woolsey,
1956-
            220.9505

ISBN 0-8280-0797-7

After Ruth's husband died, she and her mother-in-law,
Naomi, returned to Bethlehem, where Ruth helped support
Naomi by gleaning the barley left behind in Boaz's fields.
PAINTING BY RUSSELL HARLAN

CONTENTS

PART ONE—Stories of Israel in the Wilderness

PART TWO—Stories of the Conquest of Canaan

PART THREE—Stories of the Days of the Judges

PART FOUR—Stories of Samuel and Saul

PART ONE

Stories of

Israel in
the Wilderness

(Leviticus 9:1-Numbers 20:29)

Two Irreverent Young Men

(Leviticus 10:1-11)

AFTER all that had happened at the tabernacle that day when Aaron and his sons were consecrated to the priesthood, you would think that those four young men would be the last people in camp to get into trouble.

Moses himself had washed them in front of everybody. He had put those beautiful, clean clothes on them. Nadab, Abihu, Eleazar, and Ithamar had laid their hands on the calf and the ram and had confessed their sins. And blood had been placed on their ears, their right thumbs, and their right toes.

How could they have gone through all this without knowing what it meant? And if they forgot even for a moment, every time they looked at their father they could see the words "HOLY TO THE LORD."

They knew. They understood. Moses couldn't have made it more plain that God wanted them to be the best young people in the camp, an example to all the boys and girls who had come out of Egypt.

9

← PAINTING BY RUSSELL HARLAN

Aaron, assisted by his four sons, was ordained high priest to serve the people of God in their journey toward the Promised Land. His wonderful garments were most glorious to behold.

God had given Nadab, Abihu, Eleazar, and Ithamar a very wonderful opportunity. The more you think about it, the more you will see how big it really was and how much God expected of them. They were to be the spiritual leaders of the youth of Israel. They were to be young men of such spotless character and noble living that all the boys and girls would look up to them and want to be like them.

But what did they do?

Two of them got drunk. Not long after the ceremony of consecration, too.

Where they found the drink I do not know. Someone in the camp may have had a wine press, but where did they get the grapes? Someone may have known how to brew beer, but where did they get the grain? Perhaps the alcoholic beverages had been brought out of Egypt, but it's hard to think that it could have been brought through the Red Sea on the night of the great deliverance. All we know for certain is that there was alcohol of some kind in the camp, and Nadab and Abihu drank some of it.

Perhaps these two young priests didn't care very much about being chosen to work in the sanctuary. Perhaps they didn't want to be priests at all. Maybe they went through all the long consecration ceremony just because their father and uncle had told them to. The washing Moses gave them certainly didn't clean their hearts, and the blood on their toes didn't keep them from walking in wrong ways.

But their drinking was nothing compared to the crime that the drink made them commit.

Because their brains were so clouded and numbed by the alcoholic drink, they lost their sense of right and wrong and treated their sacred duties lightly. Why, they may have asked each other, did they have to light their censers at the golden altar of incense in the tabernacle? Why couldn't they light them any way they pleased? What difference would it make if they put fire in their censers themselves?

So "Aaron's sons Nadab and Abihu took their censers, put fire in them and added incense; and they offered unauthorized fire before the Lord, contrary to his command."

The two priests may even have walked unsteadily through the tabernacle, swinging their censers irreverently, with no thought of the sacred meaning of what they were supposed to be doing. We will never know exactly what they did, but God was very displeased. Not only had they disobeyed Him, but they had treated sacred things as though they were common. Though God had trusted and honored them above all the young people in the camp, they had failed Him.

God could not let disobedience and such insulting behavior like this go by unpunished. And so, as Nadab and Abihu were offering incense in the tabernacle with "unauthorized fire" in their censers, there came a flash of light from God. The two foolish youth were suddenly burned to death. The Bible says, "So fire came out from the presence of the Lord and consumed them, and they died before the Lord."

The shocking news soon spread through the camp. People were stunned to think that two of the priests who had just been consecrated to serve the Lord had been so careless.

Everybody expected there would be a big funeral for the priests, since they were Aaron's sons. But there was none. Moses would not allow it. Instead, he instructed two of the men's cousins to carry the bodies out of the camp and bury them. Moses even told Aaron and his other sons not to weep for them or show in any way that they didn't agree with God's judgment.

It must have seemed very hard to Aaron. Not only had he lost two of his sons, but he wasn't allowed to cry over them as any father would want to do.

Then the Lord spoke to him and commanded, "You and your sons are not to drink wine or other fermented drink whenever you go into the Tent of Meeting, or you will die. This is a lasting ordinance for the generations to come. You must distinguish between the holy and the common, between the unclean and the clean."

Now Aaron understood. Drink had robbed him of his sons. Drink had confused their brains so they couldn't see any difference between the holy and the unholy. Drink had led to the foolish act that had brought upon them the terrible judgment of God.

God and the Grumblers

(Numbers 10:11-11:15; 11:31-34)

NOT LONG after the death of Nadab and Abihu somebody noticed that the cloud that had hovered over the tabernacle for the past seven weeks seemed to be moving again. Word spread quickly through the camp.

"The cloud! Look at the cloud! It's moving."

It was. And it was moving toward the Promised Land. What excitement! They were going to leave Sinai at last! In a little while they would be in Canaan! It seemed too good to be true.

Eagerly the people packed up their belongings and folded their tents ready for the journey. They rounded up their cattle and sheep and harnessed their oxen to the wagons.

The Levites began to take the tabernacle apart and roll up the massive curtains. They covered the precious pieces of furniture with cloths that had been made to protect them during the trip.

Soon the whole camp was on the march, and it traveled for three days before the cloud stood still again.

Once more the Levites put up the tabernacle, and the 12 tribes camped around it.

At first the people were very happy—happier than they had been since that wonderful night when they had left Egypt. They felt that they were on their way at last. Soon they would be in Canaan, the land of their dreams.

That's what they thought, but it was not to be. They still had many lessons to learn. They had seen God's miracle at the Red Sea, they had heard His voice from Mount Sinai, and they had eaten His manna every day for many months. But they did not really love Him. Their faith in Him was still very weak.

They had not been at their new campsite for long before grumbling broke out again. Some complained about one thing, and some about another. Some didn't like the wild desert they were in and wished they were back at Sinai. Others said there wasn't enough grass for their cattle. Still others thought they had to walk too far to get water.

"Now the people complained about their hardships in the hearing of the Lord, and when he heard them his anger was aroused. Then fire from the Lord burned among them, and consumed some of the outskirts of the camp."

When the people cried to Moses for help, he prayed to God, and the fire stopped.

But even this lesson did not stop the grumbling for long. Soon it began again. Some of the other people who had come along with Israel from Egypt started it this time, but the Israelites quickly joined them. Now the trouble was food. They had grown tired of the manna and wanted meat.

"If only we had meat to eat!" they cried. "We remember the fish we ate in Egypt at no cost—also the cucumbers, melons, leeks, onions and garlic. But now we have lost our appetite; we never see anything but this manna!"

You could hear a sneer in their voices as they said "this manna," and God did not like it. He was even more displeased when they all began to cry about it, "each at the entrance to his tent."

Poor, foolish people! They could remember all the good things they had eaten in Egypt, but they had forgotten the cruel slavery they had endured, the slave drivers, the beatings, and the hard work. Yes, and they had forgotten all that God had done for them during their nearly 14 months of freedom.

Once more Moses turned to God for help. "Where can I get meat for all these people?" he said. "They keep wailing to me, 'Give us meat to eat!'"

God told him not to worry. He would see that the people got meat and that it would last them a whole month.

"But how?" asked Moses. "Here I am among six hundred thousand men on foot, and you say, 'I will give them meat to eat for a whole month!' Would they have enough if flocks and herds were slaughtered for them? Would they have enough if all the fish in the sea were caught for them?"

The Lord answered Moses, "Is the Lord's arm too short? You will now see whether or not what I say will come true for you."

Moses should have remembered that God could do what-

15

ever He promised. God had helped him out of a tight spot like this once before, soon after the Israelites had left Egypt.

The next day the wind began to blow from the Red Sea, and with it came the quails again, only this time by countless thousands. The air was thick with them. They flew in very low—"about three feet above the ground"—and as they went by, the people knocked them down with sticks or caught them with their bare hands. Every man and woman, every boy and girl, collected heaps of them.

What a feast! They had cried for meat; now they had it, all they could eat. For days and days they ate nothing but quail morning, noon, and night. They didn't bother about the manna, just the quail. And they ate quail until they were sick of the very sight of it.

Many ate so much they became ill. A plague broke out. Maybe food poisoning and overeating caused the problem. Whatever it was, hundreds died. Every day there were more and more funerals.

So many people died that this stopping place on the road to Canaan was given a new name: Kibroth Hattaavah. It's a long name, but it's worth remembering. It means "the graves of craving." That's where the greedy people were buried.

Two Missing Men

(Numbers 11:16-30)

THE ENDLESS grumbling was almost too much for Moses. And no wonder. It was hard enough to take thousands of men, women, and children through a hot, dry desert without having to put up with all their faultfinding.

When Moses prayed about it, God told him to choose 70 of the best men of Israel and form a council to take care of some of his work load. Then he wouldn't get all the blame when things seemed to go wrong.

Jethro, his father-in-law, had once told him the same thing. That was when Moses had appointed rulers over thousands, hundreds, fifties, and tens. But even so he was still killing himself with work and worry.

"Bring me seventy of Israel's elders," God said, "who are known to you as leaders and officials among the people. Have them come to the Tent of Meeting, that they may stand there with you."

Obediently Moses made out a list of the best men he knew in the camp. Then he sent word to them to meet him at the door of the tabernacle.

Strangely, only 68 came. When the roll was called, two were missing—Eldad and Medad. Their names suggest that they may have been brothers, maybe twins.

The Bible doesn't say why they didn't come when Moses called them. It couldn't have been because they were rebellious, or obstinate, or anything like that. If they *had* been, Moses would never have chosen them to be members of the new council of Israel. Probably they were doing some kind deed for somebody and couldn't leave it, or they didn't feel worthy of the honor that Moses had offered them.

Anyway, they didn't come, and Moses had to go on without them. He positioned the 68 leaders "around the Tent" and waited for God to act.

Suddenly the pillar of cloud came down very close to them all—so near that they could hear God speak to Moses.

Then something very wonderful happened. The Spirit of God came upon them all, and "they prophesied." It must have been something like Pentecost, about 1,500 years later, when the Holy Spirit came upon the disciples and they began to talk about God's wonderful things.

Now we can see why Moses placed the 68 men "around the Tent." If they had been bunched together when they all started talking at once, there would have been so much noise that no one could have understood anything. But now each man had his own audience. And as the people who had gathered around the tabernacle listened to the beautiful things the men were saying, they were impressed that Moses had chosen true men of God to be their spiritual leaders.

In the middle of all the excitement a young man pressed through the crowd and came running to Moses, crying, "Eldad and Medad are prophesying in the camp."

So God had not forgotten the two missing men, even though they hadn't been able to come to the meeting at the tabernacle. He had put His Spirit on them too, which proves that they must both have been very good men.

But Joshua didn't like what was going on. "Moses, my lord," he cried, "stop them."

Joshua was afraid that if other people began prophesying in the camp, it would take away some of Moses' power and authority.

But Moses didn't mind. "Are you jealous for my sake?" he asked. "I wish that all the Lord's people were prophets and that the Lord would put his Spirit on them!"

Moses wasn't a bit jealous because other people were beginning to do the things that he had been trying to do all by himself up to now. He was ready to share the glory of leadership, if this was God's will. Why should he worry if Eldad and Medad were prophesying in the camp? He wished everybody in Israel were worthy of the honor.

Those words of Moses, "I wish that all the Lord's people were prophets," are among the finest in the Bible. We should all try to remember them. For willingness to share the joys and rewards of leadership is a sign of real nobility. Only little, selfish people try to keep the best things, the first places, the highest honors, all to themselves.

Trouble in the Family

(Numbers 12)

THERE is an old saying that "it never rains but it pours." Certainly Moses must have thought so when not only were the people grumbling but his own brother and sister started to complain about him.

This must have been very hard for Moses to understand, because he loved Aaron and Miriam very much. Miriam was his big sister, who had watched over him when he was just a baby floating in a basket among the papyrus plants on the river Nile. Once Aaron had walked all the way from Egypt to Mount Sinai to see him. All three of them had worked and worried and prayed together over the great task of bringing Israel out of Egypt.

What could be the matter with them? They were behaving like naughty children, instead of the elderly grown-ups that they were.

First they began to tease Moses about his wife. Because she was a Midianite with dark skin, they said that she was

21

an Ethiopian, or a Cushite. There was a cruel barb in what they were saying that Moses didn't like.

Next they said, "Has the Lord spoken only through Moses? . . . Hasn't he also spoken through us?"

Ah! So this was it! They were jealous about something.

Moses wondered what it could be. Did they want his job? Were they tired of his being in charge?

Then he remembered. Of course! Like Joshua, they were unhappy about the appointment of the 70 elders and the way God's Spirit had been poured out on them. They were afraid they wouldn't be quite so important in the camp from now on. Moses, they thought, should have asked *them* before doing anything like this.

What a terrible state of affairs! If Aaron and Miriam were beginning to grumble like the others, things had become pretty bad. What could be done about it?

There was nothing Moses could do. He had just been obeying God's instructions when he had named the 70 elders. And he certainly hadn't been responsible for pouring out God's Spirit on them. But Moses wasn't the kind of man who would argue for himself. The Bible says that by this time "Moses was a very humble man, more humble than anyone else on the face of the earth."

Here was a situation where God had to step in. And He would have to settle the matter in a big way to make sure there would be no more misunderstanding. So, while the three were talking together rather heatedly, "The Lord said to Moses, Aaron and Miriam, 'Come out to the Tent of Meeting, all three of you.' " This was an order.

They went, wondering what was going to happen next. When they arrived at the tabernacle, the pillar of cloud came down very low until all three of them seemed to be shut in with God.

Then God spoke. "Aaron and Miriam," He said, and the two stepped forward. "Listen to my words: When a prophet of

the Lord is among you, I reveal myself to him in visions, I speak to him in dreams. But this is not true of my servant Moses; he is faithful in all my house. With him I speak face to face, clearly and not in riddles; he sees the form of the Lord. Why then were you not afraid to speak against my servant Moses?"

Aaron and Miriam stood silent, because it was clear that God was very displeased because of what they had said to their brother. They waited to see whether God would speak again, but He didn't. The cloud rose, and the three found themselves standing together under the brilliant desert sunshine.

Suddenly Miriam let out a scream. "Look at me!" she cried. "Look! I have leprosy!"

"Aaron turned toward her and saw that she had leprosy."

This was terribly serious, for in those days leprosy was considered a very contagious disease. Anyone with leprosy had to be banished from the camp at once.

24

TROUBLE IN THE FAMILY

It was a most touching moment. Miriam, all broken up, was weeping her heart out at her awful punishment. Aaron, sick with worry and very sorry for his part of the trouble, was pleading for forgiveness for himself and his sister. And Moses, the one Miriam had hurt most of all by her bitter complaints, was on his knees, begging God to heal her.

Perhaps never in all history was there such a pathetic family scene. And God was watching it all. His heart of love was deeply moved. He heard Moses' prayer. Miriam was healed. But He said that she should be put out of the camp for seven days like anyone else who had leprosy. Then she could come back, and everything would be all right again.

So poor Miriam was led to the edge of the camp and put outside. Moses and Aaron went along to comfort her and tell her goodbye. And I am sure they were at the same spot a week later to welcome her back with open arms.

So Near and Yet So Far

(Numbers 13:1-14:35)

DO YOU know how far it is from Mount Sinai to the border of Canaan? Less than 150 miles (240 kilometers)! If there had been a good modern road across the desert in those days—which there wasn't—and if Israel had owned a few hundred trucks—which they didn't— they could have covered the whole distance in four or five hours.

But even the way things were—moving no faster than the littlest lamb, or the youngest child, or the most stubborn donkey—the caravan was only 11 traveling days away from the Promised Land.

It couldn't have been very long after all the trouble over the quail, and the worse trouble between Moses, Aaron, and Miriam, that they traveled close enough to see the land of their dreams. Here at last, just about 15 months after their great deliverance from Egypt, they caught their first glimpse of the green hills and fertile valleys of their future home.

How excited everyone was! I can imagine mothers hugged their children for joy at the very thought that the hard, trying days in the wilderness, with all the heat, the thirst, and the weariness, would soon be over. Boys and girls shouted for joy as they pictured the land flowing with "milk and honey" that they had heard their fathers talk about. Imagine! All the milk they could drink! All the honey they could eat! What a land it must be!

Then the people were told to rest in camp while 12 men, one from each tribe, went ahead to explore the country and find out what would have to be done to take possession of it.

These men were to spread out all over the country and learn how many people lived there, how strongly their cities were fortified, what sort of food they were growing, and whether there were any trees for lumber.

It was a great honor to be chosen for this mission. Each tribe sent its best man, a leader in Israel. A great deal depended on them—more than they knew!

The tribe of Judah sent Caleb, and the tribe of Ephraim sent

27

Joshua. There were 10 others, whose names the Bible mentions but no one remembers today.

As the 12 started out on their trip, many came to tell them goodbye and wish them well. Then, when the last man had disappeared from view, the rest went back to their tents to wait for the spies to return.

A week passed. Two weeks. Three weeks. Still there was no word. What could have happened? Had all 12 men been killed by the Canaanites? Four weeks. Five weeks—how long the waiting time seemed! Then on the fortieth day, they came back.

The spies were loaded down with various kinds of fruit. And how good it must have tasted to people who had lived in a desert so long! But the object that caught everyone's eye was a bunch of grapes so large that it took two men to carry it. If this was the produce of Canaan, what a wonderful place it must be!

The spies said they had never seen such a country. "We went into the land to which you sent us," they told the company of people gathered close about them, "and it does flow with milk and honey! Here is its fruit." The people listening were so happy that their faces were wreathed in smiles. Everyone wanted to go to the Promised Land at once.

Then came the bad news. "But the people who live there are powerful, and the cities are fortified and very large. We even saw descendants of Anak there." As some of the spies continued to describe how strong the people of Canaan were

29

The twelve spies sent to spy out the land of Canaan came back after a long time with wonderful samples of the fruit they had found there. The people rejoiced at their story.

and how difficult it would be to take the land away from them, the hearts of the Israelites sank. It was an awful blow to them.

They had thought everything was going to be easy, just like the falling of the manna and the quails being blown in by the wind. But this—this was terrible. Once again they began to grumble and complain.

But "Caleb silenced the people before Moses and said, 'We should go up and take possession of the land, for we can certainly do it.' "

It was a brave thing to say just then because all the rest of the spies, except for Joshua, were against him. The other 10 spies cried out, "We can't attack those people; they are stronger than we are."

It was two against 10—and the people believed the 10. They gave up hope of ever entering Canaan and lost themselves in despair. "That night all the people of the community raised their voices and wept aloud."

30

By the next morning they were all in a bad mood, seething with hatred of Moses and God, and full of open rebellion. "If only we had died in Egypt! Or in this desert! . . ." they cried. "We should choose a leader and go back to Egypt."

The disappointment was almost more than they could bear. But at that moment Caleb and Joshua stood up in front of the raging throng and cried, "The land we passed through and explored is exceedingly good. If the Lord is pleased with us, he will lead us into that land, a land flowing with milk and honey, and will give it to us."

"Stone them! Stone them!" cried the people.

But no one threw any stones. Suddenly the glory of the Lord appeared in the tabernacle, and the angry crowd was hushed. Israel waited, ashamed and afraid, to hear what God would say.

They didn't have long to wait. When God spoke, they saw what an awful mistake they had made.

They had said they wished they had died in the wilderness. All right, God said, they would have their wish. "Not one of the men who saw my glory and the miraculous signs I performed in Egypt and in the desert but who disobeyed me and tested me ten times—not one of them will ever see the land I promised on oath to their forefathers. No one who has treated me with contempt will ever see it. . . . They will meet their end in this desert; here they will die."

Back to the wilderness! Shut out of Canaan forever. The heartbreak of it! What a terrible price for failing to trust God!

The Great Rebellion

(*Numbers 14:36-45; 16*)

YOU CAN imagine how the people felt. They must have been hopelessly discouraged. I can almost hear the children asking their mothers, "Aren't we going to get the milk and honey today?"

"No, darlings, not today," the heartbroken mothers replied, "not for many, many days."

Then the children cried too.

Some of the men climbed a mountain peak to look again at the land they had hoped for and dreamed about so long. It seemed so near that they thought it was a shame to leave it and go back into the desert.

"Look, we are already so close," they said to one another. "Let's just go into the land the Lord promised to give us."

But it was too late. Moses heard about their plan, and he told them not to try it. "Do not go up, because the Lord is not with you," he said. "You will be defeated by your enemies, for the Amalekites and Canaanites will face you there. Because you have turned away from the Lord, he will not be with you and you will fall by the sword."

But they went anyway. Singing and shouting to keep up their courage, they marched across the border. But they never captured even the first hill. The people who lived there came and drove them out.

It was a very sorry group of men who returned to the camp that night. They knew now that it was no use trying to go into Canaan. Their last hope had gone.

Soon almost the whole camp was talking angrily about Moses. Why should they have to listen to that old man? What a mess he had made of everything! He had taken 15 months for a journey that should have been over in two weeks. And now that they had reached the border of Canaan at last, he wanted them to go back into the dreadful desert for another 38 years. Absurd! They wouldn't do it. Why should they? Who was Moses anyway?

The great rebellion was on.

The leader was Korah, a cousin of Moses and about the

same age. He may even have looked like Moses, for both had the same grandfather—Kohath, the son of Levi. Perhaps this was one reason why so many others were ready to follow him. Anyway, he stirred up no less than "250 Israelite men, well-known community leaders who had been appointed members of the council," and together they marched up to Moses and Aaron.

"You have gone too far!" they said insolently. "The whole community is holy, and the Lord is with them. Why then do you set yourselves above the Lord's assembly?"

"You Levites have gone too far," Moses told them, using their own words. Then he explained to them that he was willing to let God decide who should be the leader.

"Take censers," he ordered, "and tomorrow put fire and incense in them before the Lord. The man the Lord chooses will be the one who is holy."

Then Moses sent messengers to get the other two conspirators, Dathan and Abiram, members of the tribe of Reuben. But they refused to come. Instead, they sent back this disrespecful message: "Isn't it enough that you have brought us up out of a land flowing with milk and honey to kill us in the desert? And now you also want to lord it over us? Moreover, you haven't brought us into a land flowing with milk and honey or given us an inheritance of fields and vineyards. Will you gouge out the eyes of these men? No, we will not come!"

No one had ever talked to Moses like this before, and he was very angry. To think that they spoke of Egypt as a land flowing with milk and honey—Egypt, the land of their slavery!

And to think they would suggest that he wanted to be a dictator who would put out the eyes of those who disagreed with him!

"Lord!" he cried in his anger and sorrow, "I have not taken so much as a donkey from them, nor have I wronged any of them."

Showdown time had come. God's whole plan of salvation was in danger. If the rebels won, all He had tried to do for Israel would be lost.

That night the whole camp was filled with excited rumors. Bitter, angry words were spoken in hundreds of tents. Friends of Korah, Dathan, and Abiram went everywhere, urging everybody to meet at the tabernacle in the morning to see the end of Moses and his tyranny.

Early the next morning, as the people were marching toward the tabernacle, God said to Moses and Aaron, " 'Separate yourselves from this assembly so I can put an end to them at once.' But Moses and Aaron fell facedown and cried out, 'O God, God of the spirits of all mankind, will you be angry with the entire assembly when only one man sins?' "

In this moment of crisis these two dear old men prayed for the very people who were plotting against them! Then Moses strode through the gathering crowd to the tent where Korah, Dathan, and Abiram were meeting.

"Stand back, stand back!" he called to the seething throng of onlookers. "Move back from the tents of these wicked men! Do not touch anything belonging to them, or you will be swept away because of all their sins."

A great silence fell as he spoke again. "This is how you will know that the Lord has sent me to do all these things and that it was not my idea: If these men die a natural death and experience only what usually happens to men, then the Lord has not sent me. But if the Lord brings about something totally new, and the earth opens its mouth and swallows them, with everything that belongs to them, and they go down alive into the grave, then you will know that these men have treated the Lord with contempt."

"Now we know he has gone too far!" some said. "Does Moses think he can make the earth open to swallow his enemies?"

Hardly had they spoken when there was a terrible roar and the earth did open—right where Korah, Dathan, and Abiram were standing. Suddenly all three of them "went down alive into the grave, with everything they owned; the earth closed over them."

Shrieks filled the air as the people fled in panic. Then sheets of flame swept around the 250 men with the fire-filled censers, and they were burned to death. You would think that this would have been enough to convince everybody as to who was right and who was wrong, but no.

36

THE GREAT REBELLION

"You have killed the Lord's people!" shouted the friends of the rebels. A mob gathered and started after Moses and Aaron. But as it moved toward the tabernacle, people began to fall down, right and left, all through the crowd.

"Wrath has come out from the Lord," Moses cried out in alarm. "The plague has started." Even with a bloodthirsty mob coming after him, Moses was more anxious for the lives of his people than for his own life. "Take your censer and put incense in it, along with fire from the altar," he cried to Aaron, "and hurry to the assembly to make atonement for them."

Aaron went. With his smoking censer in his hand he "ran into the midst of the assembly."

Imagine it! The kindly old man, 85 years of age, running this way and that, waving his censer and crying to God to spare the people who had done so great a wrong!

What wonderful love! The Bible says that Aaron "stood between the living and the dead, and the plague stopped."

Flowers on a Stick

(Numbers 17)

THE GREAT rebellion was over. Nearly 15,000 people had died in the plague, 250 leaders had been burned by the fire, and the families of Korah, Dathan, and Abiram had disappeared when the earth opened and swallowed them up. The rest were badly frightened and thankful to be alive.

The trouble had erupted because the people were so disappointed at being told they could not enter Canaan for another 38 years. But the rebellion had been brewing for a long time. Korah might have been jealous of his cousin Aaron from the moment Aaron was made high priest. By talking against Aaron to other Levites, he probably had thought he might someday get Aaron's job. Dathan and Abiram had been jealous of Moses because he was leader and they were not. So they too had stirred up trouble until open rebellion had broken out.

Now they were gone. But had those who were left learned their lesson? Did they all agree now that God wanted Moses and

Aaron to lead them? It looked like it for the moment, but who could be quite sure? Because so many Levites had been severely punished, perhaps many were wondering whether God had rejected them as caretakers of the tabernacle.

To help make His wishes plain, God told Moses to tell the leaders of the 12 tribes to come to the tabernacle. Each was to bring his staff with him—the long stick men carried in those days when they went walking.

The 12 men came. Aaron was with them, as head of the tribe of Levi. They all must have wondered why Moses had sent for them. No doubt they suspected that it might have something to do with the sad events of the past few days.

Imagine their surprise when Moses asked them to hand him their staffs. Whatever could he want with them? As each leader handed over his staff, Moses carefully wrote the man's name on it before placing it with the others. This must have taken some time, and as they waited, the men wondered and wondered what was going to happen next.

When all 12 names had been written so clearly that there could be no possible mistake, Moses gathered all the staffs in his arms and carried them into the tabernacle. When he came out again, he told the men that they could go but that they were to come back the next day.

Moses explained that God would show them by a miracle which of the tribes he had chosen to conduct the services of the sanctuary and which man was His chosen leader. The sign would be the blossoming of this man's staff. Buds and flowers would appear on the dry old stick.

The men were excited as they returned to their tents. Perhaps, they thought, God would make a change in the leadership of Israel, and this was His way of telling them. Someone other than Aaron might be high priest tomorrow. Which of them would it be?

As they went on their way people must have noticed that they had no staffs.

"Have you lost your staffs?" they asked.

"Oh, no, we all left them at the tabernacle," they replied. "We are waiting to see which one of them will blossom and bear fruit."

The next morning a crowd gathered at the tabernacle to learn the result. Which, if any, of the staffs had blossomed?

When the 12 leaders had arrived, Moses went into the tabernacle. Even he was surprised at what he saw, for one of the staffs not only had buds and blossoms on it, but ripe almonds as well.

40

Then Moses brought the staffs outside. You can imagine how astonished everybody was when they saw that one of them had turned into a tree overnight.

"Whose staff is it?" they cried.

"Come and see," said Moses.

The 12 men eagerly pressed forward. Then they saw the name. It was quite clear and unmistakable, in spite of all the blossoms and the almonds around it.

"Aaron!" they said.

So there was to be no change in leadership after all. And they were all satisfied, for no one could doubt that God had spoken. Clearly He still wanted the tribe of Levi to care for the tabernacle, and Aaron to be high priest.

Aaron was the only man who didn't get his staff back. God told Moses to take it into the tabernacle and keep it there "as a sign to the rebellious" and to "put an end to their grumbling."

And it did take away their murmuring for a while, but not for very long. All too soon they were complaining again.

Water From a Rock

(Numbers 20:1-13)

FOR THE next 38 years the children of Israel wandered in the desert. We don't know very much about what happened to them during that time. Slowly, wearily, they moved from place to place, staying just long enough for the cattle to eat what little grass they could find. Then on they went again, scorched by the blistering sun and with no clear purpose or hope.

It was enough to break their hearts. Many times they must have thought they were paying an awful price for their lack of faith in God. But God chose this way to show them—and all who came after them—just how important it is to believe and act on His word.

One by one all who had taken part in the great rebellion died. Before the 38 years had passed, at least 600 thousand graves dotted the cruel and lonely desert.

But even though God allowed His people to suffer, He didn't leave them. Every day, except the seventh day of each week, He sent them manna to eat. Every day, from the moment

Moses struck the rock in Horeb soon after they came out of Egypt, there was water for them to drink. It didn't follow them all the way from Horeb, but it always came bubbling up out of the rocky soil just when they needed it the most.

The prophet Isaiah wrote many years later, "They did not thirst when he led them through the deserts; he made water flow for them from the rock; he split the rock and the water gushed out." [1] David recalled that "like a river it flowed in the desert." [2]

Then one day as their years of wandering came to an end, the flow of water stopped. If they had carefully counted the years of their punishment, they should have taken this as a sign that it was almost time for them to enter Canaan. But they didn't. Instead, once more they came grumbling to Moses and Aaron—now two very old men.

"If only we had died when our brothers fell dead before the Lord!" they wailed. "Why did you bring the Lord's community into this desert, that we and our livestock should die here? Why did you bring us up out of Egypt to this terrible place? It has no grain or figs, grapevines or pomegranates. And there is no water to drink!"

It was the same old story, the same old complaint. Just as soon as things began to go wrong, they wished they were back in Egypt and blamed Moses for all their troubles.

Just as they had done so many times before, Moses and Aaron turned to God for help. Going to the door of the tabernacle, they fell upon their faces. "And the glory of the Lord appeared to them." They might be old, but God was still the same as ever, still ready to show them the way out of their problems.

"Gather the assembly together," God told Moses and Aaron. "Speak to that rock before their eyes. . . . You will bring water out of the rock for the community."

So Moses and Aaron called all the people to come to the great rock that towered above the camp. Standing beneath it, Moses cried, "Listen, you rebels, must *we* bring you water out of this rock?"

That is where Moses made a big mistake. He forgot to give God the glory for the miracle. Then he made another mistake. He "raised his arm and struck the rock twice with his staff."

Water gushed out of the rock. The people, overjoyed, stooped down to drink, and the thirsty cattle came running toward the cool, sparkling stream. Moses and Aaron stood alone—in disgrace.

"Because you did not trust in me enough to honor me as holy in the sight of the Israelites," God told them, "you will not bring this community into the land I give them."

The hearts of the two old men sank. They couldn't go into Canaan? After all that they had done for Israel, after all the trials they had endured, after all the long, long journey they had traveled? Surely God didn't mean that! How could He? What had they done to deserve so great a punishment?

They had spoiled something very beautiful. They had ruined an important lesson that God wanted to teach not only to Israel but to people in all the world.

The rock was a symbol of Christ. He was to be struck once, but never again. He was to be "sacrificed *once* to take away the sins of many,"³ not sacrificed many times, over and over again.

Moses had struck the rock once—at Horeb. That was right. He had been told to do that. But now he had struck it again, twice, in fact. And God had told him to *speak* to it—not to strike it—just as sinners may speak to Christ anywhere, whenever they need Him, and bring the water of life into their souls.

Poor Moses and Aaron! Maybe they didn't understand all this as we do now. God didn't blame them for failing to understand but for failing to believe and obey. 🖋

¹ Isaiah 48:21.
² Psalm 105:41.
³ Hebrews 9:28.

A Sad Farewell

(Numbers 20:14-29)

T HE NEWS that he couldn't enter Canaan was hard for Moses to take. He was terribly disappointed. Who wouldn't have been? But give up? Never! He had known God too well to doubt His goodness and love. As long as he had life and health he would serve God faithfully and lead Israel toward the Promised Land.

Forgetting himself, Moses began to plan the next step of the journey. He had made up his mind that the easiest way to get to Canaan was through the land of Edom. He sent messengers to the king of that country, asking permission for Israel to pass through.

It was a very kind and friendly message, because the Edomites were also descendants of Abraham, through Esau. After telling the king about some of the hard times Israel had suffered, Moses wrote, "Please let us pass through your country. We will not go through any field or vineyard, or drink water from any well. We will travel along the king's highway and not turn to the right or to the left until we have passed through your territory."

But the king of Edom said No. "You may not pass through here," he replied. "If you try, we will march out and attack you with the sword."

It was a cruel, selfish answer, but Moses refused to get angry about it. Instead, he sent another gracious note, assuring the king that Israel would keep to the mountain roads and pay for any water—even from the streams—that they might drink on their way through.

But still the king of Edom refused, and Israel had to find another way to get to Canaan.

Moving on east and south to get around Edom, they came to Mount Hor.

A very sad thing happened here. As the people pitched camp God told Moses that Aaron was going to die. He wanted both of them to climb to the top of the mountain and take Eleazar, Aaron's son, with them.

It must have been a sorrowful little procession that made its way slowly—so very slowly—up the mountainside. Aaron was 123 years old, and Moses was just three years younger. They had been friends such a long, long time and had stood together through all sorts of troubles. Now they were to be separated.

I suppose they stopped many times on the way, just so they could talk a little longer and make the final walk together last as long as possible. But little by little, step by weary step, they came near the top. Looking down, they saw the camp of Israel spread out on the plain below. Perhaps they told each other how much those poor, dear people meant to them and how they had tried so hard to help them.

A few more steps brought them to the top of the mountain. Then something very touching took place. One by one Moses removed Aaron's high priestly garments, placing each one on Eleazar as tears flowed down all their cheeks. It was time to say goodbye to each other.

"Goodbye, son; God bless you."

"Goodbye, Father."

Then the two brothers looked into each other's eyes for

the last time. "Farewell!" they said. And Aaron breathed his last, his brother's arms around him.

In the camp far below, the people began to get worried. Why were Moses, Aaron, and Eleazar staying on the mountain so long?

Then, looking up, they saw two figures coming down the winding path. Aaron was not with them, and his son Eleazar was wearing his high priestly robes.

Quickly they guessed what had happened, and the sad message swept through the camp—"Aaron is dead!"

Though some had not liked him and some had quarreled with him, now they all felt sorry he was gone. And "the entire house of Israel mourned for him thirty days."

PART TWO

Stories of

the Conquest of Canaan

(Numbers 21:1-Joshua 24:33)

Snake on a Pole

(Numbers 21:4-9)

A MONTH after Aaron's death Moses ordered the children of Israel to take down the camp and move on once more. He knew there wasn't much time left now. The years of wandering in the wilderness were almost over.

Other people in the camp had been counting those years, too. Since the great rebellion of Korah, Dathan, and Abiram, thousands of boys had grown to manhood, and girls to womanhood. They had married and had children of their own in that hot, dry, desolate land. For months and months they had waited, longing for the day when they would be allowed to enter Canaan.

How slowly the years had gone by! Ten, 20, 30—each one marked by more and more funerals as the old folks who had left Egypt passed away. It must have seemed that the 38 years of wandering would never end.

Thirty-five, 36, 37, 38. At last the time was drawing near.

But then the people had a big disappointment. As the long

caravan began to move onward again, they noticed that instead of going due north, they were traveling southeast "along the route to the Red Sea, to go around Edom."

This was too much. They didn't want to see the Red Sea anymore. They wanted to go to Canaan by the shortest and quickest way possible. The thought of having to backtrack again almost broke their hearts. The Bible says that they "grew impatient on the way." It seemed to them as though they might miss the Promised Land after all.

Grumbling broke out once more. "They spoke against God and against Moses," saying, "Why have you brought us up out of Egypt to die in the desert? There is no bread! There is no water! And we detest this miserable food!"

For a while it looked as if there might be another great rebellion, but suddenly something happened that changed everything. Poisonous snakes appeared all over the desert. They crawled into the tents, into the bedding, into the wagons, into the food supplies. They were all over the place. It was terrifying. Many people were bitten and died.

Some tried to kill the snakes, but the more they killed,

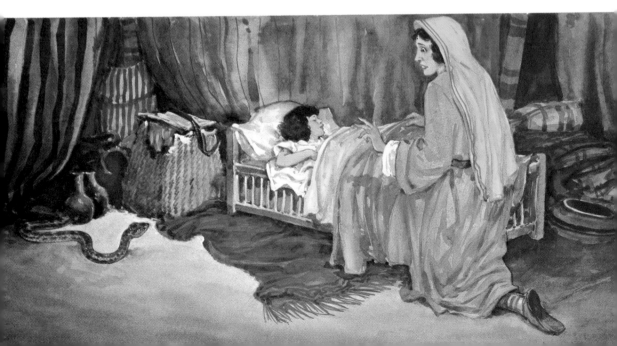

it seemed, the more appeared. There wasn't anything they could do to get rid of the snakes. The people were so afraid they couldn't eat or sleep.

At last the people came to Moses and begged for help. " 'We sinned when we spoke against the Lord and against you. Pray that the Lord will take the snakes away from us.' So Moses prayed for the people."

Then the Lord directed Moses to do a strange thing. Instead of telling him how to get rid of the snakes, He told him how to cure the people who had been bitten.

"Make a snake," God said, "and put it up on a pole; anyone who is bitten can look at it and live."

"So Moses made a bronze snake and put it up on a pole. Then when anyone was bitten by a snake and looked at the bronze snake, he lived."

A wonderful thing happened then. As the dying people looked at the bronze snake, happy cries of "I'm cured! I'm cured!" rose from every part of the camp. Just looking at the snake on the pole completely healed them.

I can see a mother holding her little boy in her arms. She is desperately worried about him, for he is very ill. The poison is killing him. In a few more minutes he'll be dead. She tries to get him to look at the bronze snake on the pole.

"Look, darling, look!" she cries frantically.

"Look at what?" the poor boy asks weakly.

"The snake, the bronze snake! Just look over there. See it hanging up on that pole?"

Slowly the boy turns his head. A smile spreads over his face. The pain has gone. He feels better at once.

Scenes like this were taking place all through the camp. The children of Israel were learning an important lesson—the power of faith in the word of God. It wasn't the bronze snake that helped them. Not at all. A bronze snake couldn't help anybody, any more than a bronze elephant or a bronze billy goat could. But when they did exactly as God told them, and *looked* at the snake, their faith brought His power

into their lives, and they were healed.

The children of Israel kept this bronze snake for a long, long time. As the years rolled by, however, they forgot its true meaning and made an idol of it. They even burned incense to it as though it were a god. Centuries later, good king Hezekiah destroyed it. Then it was called "Nehushtan," [1] meaning "a piece of bronze." And that's all it was, just a piece of bronze that couldn't help or heal anybody.

Hundreds of years afterward Jesus said to Nicodemus, "Just as Moses lifted up the snake in the desert, so the Son of Man must be lifted up, that everyone who believes in him may have eternal life." [2]

This is one of the most beautiful things Jesus ever said. He was "lifted up" on the cross of Calvary. Ever since then, thousands of people in every land have looked to Him in faith and have been saved from the curse of sin.

His promise still stands. It is for you and for me. It is for every boy and every girl in the whole wide world.

Today, if you are bitten by "that ancient serpent, who is the devil, or Satan," [3] turn your eyes upon Jesus. Think about His cross. Remember His promise that "*whoever* believes in him shall not perish but have eternal life." [4] And the life of God, with all its healing, cleansing, forgiving power, will flow into your life.

---

[1] 2 Kings 18:4.
[2] John 3:14, 15.
[3] Revelation 20:2.
[4] John 3:16.

57

← PAINTING BY HARRY ANDERSON

All who looked at the brazen serpent were healed from the bite of poisonous snakes. The story was to remind us of Jesus' power to save when we look to Him for help.

The Talking Donkey

(Numbers 21:16-35; 22; 23; 24)

FROM the moment that the children of Israel began to trust God, as they did when they looked at the snake on the pole, things began to go better for them.

Coming to the end of the desert, they were glad to see the green, fertile land. Then Moses did something different from anything he had ever done before. He told the princes of Israel to dig a well with their staffs!

Did you ever try to dig a hole in sand with a round stick? How far down did you get?

All the people gathered to watch the princes at work, and everybody was smiling. (Just imagine how you would feel if you saw the leaders of your church trying to dig a hole with long sticks!) Of course they didn't get anywhere.

But wonder of wonders, water came bubbling up out of the very sand they had been trying so hard to move! Again God let them see that He was able and willing to provide for them, even when they could do so little for themselves.

When they saw the water, the people began to sing, and

their song ran like this, "Spring up, O well! Sing about it."

They were happy now. Here was new proof that God was with them. From their faith came happiness, and from happiness, their first victories.

Moving north, they asked Sihon, king of the Amorites, for permission to pass through his country. He refused, even though they promised not to go into his fields or his vineyards, but to "travel along the king's highway." Sihon marched against them with all his soldiers, but Israel won the battle, sweeping on to take all his cities from the river Arnon up to the river Jabbok.

If you will look on the map on page 106, you will see that the river Arnon runs into the Dead Sea and the river Jabbok into the river Jordan. This will give you an idea how much land the children of Israel took from the Amorites and how they went up *east* of the Dead Sea to get to Canaan.

Og, king of Bashan, was the next to fight Israel. He was a giant, and his people lived in a rocky mountain fortress. But he was defeated too, and Israel took all his land.

By this time the rulers of other cities began to be afraid of Israel. Balak, king of the Moabites, was so scared that he said to his friends the Midianites, "This horde [meaning Israel] is going to lick up everything around us, as an ox

59

licks up the grass of the field."

Then Balak had a bright idea. If he couldn't fight with Israel, perhaps he could get some sorcerer to curse them, weakening them so much that he could drive them out of the land.

Balak thought of a man named Balaam, who was supposed to be able to do this sort of thing. But Balaam lived in Mesopotamia, 400 miles (650 kilometers) away. Should Balak send so far away for help?

It seemed to be the only way out. Israel was a deadly menace to his country. So Balak sent messengers with a large sum of money to persuade Balaam to come.

"Look at what's happened to me," he said in his message to Balaam. "A people has come out of Egypt; they cover the face of the land and have settled next to me. Now come and put a curse on these people, because they are too powerful for me."

Balaam listened to what the messengers had to say, but God told him not to go. So Balaam refused to return with them to Balak. The messengers went all the way back to the land of Moab without him.

When Balak saw that Balaam hadn't come with his messengers, he was very upset. He chose some of the most important men in his country and sent them back to Balaam. They carried with them more money than before, and they promised Balaam great honors if he would just come and curse Israel.

Even though Balaam knew that God didn't want him to go, he told the messengers that he would ask again. This dis-

pleased God, but He told Balaam he could go. So Balaam saddled up his donkey and "went with the princes of Moab."

It wasn't an easy trip. Not only was it a very long journey and a very hot one, but unknown to Balaam, an angel had been sent from heaven to warn him about cursing Israel. As for that donkey he was riding—well, Balaam never dreamed that it could see angels and talk!

The first that Balaam knew anything was wrong was when the donkey ran right off the trail into a field. This made Balaam look foolish in front of his two servants and the princes of Moab. He was very annoyed. Of course, he didn't know that the donkey had seen an angel waving a sword. So he hit the poor animal, forcing it back onto the path.

Some distance down the road, the donkey balked again. They were going along a narrow path between two vineyards. There was a wall on either side, and suddenly the donkey shied and crushed Balaam's foot against the wall. Again Balaam was very angry, and he struck the donkey a cruel blow.

As they traveled on, they came to a very narrow place, perhaps on the edge of a cliff, "where there was no room to turn, either to the right or to the left." The donkey saw the angel again, and it lay right down under Balaam. This made him more angry than ever, and he beat the donkey with a stick.

To his astonishment Balaam heard a voice that nobody ever heard before or since. The donkey began speaking! No one knows what her voice sounded like, but I'd like to have heard it, wouldn't you?

"What have I done to you," asked the donkey, "to make you beat me these three times?"

"You have made a fool of me!" said Balaam, angry that his animal had behaved so badly before such important people. "If I had a sword in my hand, I would kill you right now."

"Am I not your own donkey," said the poor little animal, "which you have always ridden, to this day? Have I been in the habit of doing this to you?"

"No," agreed Balaam reluctantly.

"Then the Lord opened Balaam's eyes," and he saw what the donkey had seen all along—"the angel of the Lord standing in the road with his sword."

Instantly Balaam fell flat on his face.

And what do you suppose the angel said to him first? He spoke about the poor little donkey, showing how God cares for animals.

"Why have you beaten your donkey these three times? I have come here to oppose you because your path is a reckless one before me. The donkey saw me and turned away from me these three times. If she had not turned away, I would certainly have killed you by now, but I would have spared her."

"I have sinned," said Balaam. He offered to go back home right away.

But the angel said, "Go with the men, but speak only what I tell you."

So Balaam went on with the princes to Moab. Overjoyed at his arrival, King Balak took Balaam to a mountain peak where they could both look down on the camp of Israel. "Now curse them for me," he said.

But Balaam couldn't do it. Instead, he blessed them.

Balak, annoyed, took him to another place, then another, but it was no use. Balaam couldn't think of a single curse. He just said what God told him to say, and it was all blessing.

"May those who bless you be blessed," he said of Israel, "and those who curse you be cursed!"

This made Balak very angry, as you can imagine. "I summoned you to curse my enemies," he cried, thinking of all the money he had promised to pay Balaam and of the princes he'd sent to coax him, "but you have blessed them these three times. Now leave at once and go home!"

Balaam left—as fast as his little donkey would carry him.

I wonder what the donkey said to him on the way back. Wouldn't we all like to know!

Five Young Women Make History

(Numbers 26; 27:1-11; 36:1-12)

ISRAEL was now camped on the east of the river Jordan, right across from the city of Jericho. It was nearly time for them to enter Canaan, and every able-bodied man would be needed for the invasion. So God told Moses to count the people and find out just how many there were.

Nearly 40 years earlier, the number of men 20 years old and older was 603,550. Now the count was 601,730. This gives some idea of the awful number of deaths that took place in the desert. All but two of the 603,550 died—everyone except Caleb and Joshua.

When the men in charge of the numbering were counting the tribe of Manasseh, they got as far as Zelophehad and stopped. Zelophehad, a great-great-grandson of Joseph, was dead and he had five daughters, but no sons.

In those days after a man died, his belongings usually went to his sons. Since Zelophehad didn't have any sons, his daughters were afraid that they would be overlooked when

Caanan was divided up among the Israelite families. They didn't like that idea. Not a bit! And they decided to do something about it.

There must have been something very striking about these five young women, because they are mentioned by name several times in the Bible. Perhaps you should learn their names so you won't forget them. Here they are: Mahlah, Noah, Hoglah, Milcah, and Tirzah. These girls really made history.

First of all, they asked to see Moses. He agreed to meet them and hear their story. When they went to the tabernacle to keep the appointment, whom do you suppose they saw? Not only was Moses waiting to greet them, but also Eleazar (the new high priest), all the princes of the congregation, and almost everybody else in camp!

Bravely the five girls walked into the middle of that huge crowd, right up to the door of the tabernacle. What courage they had! Girls had never dared to do anything like that before.

I don't know just which one was the speaker. Mahlah was the oldest. She might have spoken for her sisters, but even she must have been quite young, because none of them were married yet. Whoever it was who spoke, she presented their case in a sensible manner.

"Our father died in the desert," she explained. "He was not among Korah's followers, who banded together against the Lord, but he died for his own sin and left no sons. Why should our father's name disappear from his clan because he had no son? Give us property among our father's relatives."

Moses listened patiently. It seemed to him that the request was fair. But before deciding, he said he would talk to God about it.

God answered Moses by saying, "What Zelophehad's daughters are saying is right. You must certainly give them property as an inheritance among their father's relatives and turn their father's inheritance over to them."

He added, "Say to the Israelites, 'If a man dies and leaves no son, turn his inheritance over to his daughter.' "

The law of inheritance given by God at that time is very similar to inheritance laws used in many countries today. These five girls made history by standing up for something they believed to be right. Their brave example has been a blessing to girls—and boys—down through the ages from that day to this.

You'll be glad to learn that all five young women got married. The Bible says so. "Zelophehad's daughters— Mahlah, Tirzah, Hoglah, Milcah and Noah—married their cousins on their father's side." It seems like the story should end by saying, "And they lived happily ever after." Of course it doesn't, but I'm sure they lived happily for a long, long time.

66

Lonely Journey

(Deuteronomy 1-34)

PLEASE, please, dear Lord, let me go over and see the land of Canaan," Moses prayed over and over again.

And no wonder! For 80 years he had dreamed about it. During those dark days in Egypt and all through the years of wandering in the desert, he had thought about it. When the people had become discouraged, he had tried to cheer them up with stories of the good things they would enjoy in the Land of Promise.

Now Moses and the Israelites had arrived at the Jordan. Across the river he could see Jericho and the mountains beyond. He was so near, and yet so far!

Again he cried to God, "Let me go over and see the good land beyond the Jordan—that fine hill country and Lebanon."

But again God said No. "Do not speak to me anymore about this matter," He said.

It must have been hard to take. And all because of

that one sin when he had disobeyed God and hit the rock twice. But even though God's refusal to allow him to go into Canaan meant giving up one of the sweetest dreams of his life, Moses knew God loved him. And he loved God so dearly that he was willing to do whatever He asked.

"Go up to the top of Pisgah," God said to him, "and look west and north and south and east. Look at the land with your own eyes, since you are not going to cross this Jordan. But commission Joshua, and encourage and strengthen him, for he will lead this people across and will cause them to inherit the land that you will see."

Moses knew now that his end was near. The time had come for Israel to cross the Jordan, and he must be left behind. They would go on, and he would stay. Joshua would lead them, not he.

So Moses called the people together for the last time. They came flocking to him, as they had done so many times before.

Standing before the vast congregation, he spoke in a voice as loud and clear as ever, for though he was old, "his eyes were not weak nor his strength gone." Hour after hour he retold the story of God's blessings through the 40 years since the great deliverance from Egypt.

Most of those who listened had never seen Egypt. Some had been just boys and girls, or babies in their mothers' arms, at the crossing of the Red Sea. Many had only a faint memory of the giving of the law on Mount Sinai. As for the children, all they knew about these things was what their parents had told them.

So Moses began at the beginning and told the whole wonderful story over again, reminding them of the way God had sent them food and water and given them victory.

"The Lord your God carried you, as a father carries his son," he said, "all the way you went."

They all understood that, especially the smaller boys and girls. They remembered how their daddies picked them up when they were tired and put them on their shoulders.

God had been like a father to them all, helping them every time they needed Him. And why? Because He wanted them to be a good example to all other people in the world. He gave them the Ten Commandments so that they would know the difference between right and wrong. He told them to build a sanctuary so that they would know that God expected them to be a pure and holy people.

"For you are a people holy to the Lord your God," said Moses. "The Lord your God has chosen you out of all the

69

peoples on the face of the earth to be his people, his treasured possession."

Then he added, so they wouldn't have any wrong ideas, "The Lord did not set his affection on you and choose you because you were more numerous than other peoples, for you were the fewest of all peoples. But it was because the Lord loved you and kept the oath he swore to your forefathers that he brought you out with a mighty hand . . . from the power of Pharaoh king of Egypt."

God loved them so much that there was nothing He would not do for them, if only they would be true to Him. "All these blessings will come upon you and accompany you if you obey the Lord your God."

All sorts of blessings would come running after them, catch up with them, and surprise them. They would be blessed in their cities and on their farms, at home and abroad, everywhere and in everything. "The Lord will open the heavens, the storehouse of his bounty, to send rain on your land in season and to bless all the work of your hands. You will lend to many nations but will borrow from none. The Lord will make you the head, not the tail."

Moses tried to tell them how much good would come to them if they would keep close to God and remember to obey Him. But he also warned them of what would happen if they should forget God and turn away from Him. Instead of being blessed, they would be cursed. Sickness, disease, and trouble of

70

all kinds would come upon them. Instead of enjoying the Promised Land, they would be scattered among all nations.

"If you do not carefully follow all the words of this law, which are written in this book," he said, "and do not revere this glorious and awesome name—the Lord your God—the Lord will send fearful plagues on you. . . . Then the Lord will scatter you among all nations, from one end of the earth to the other."

Closing his talk, he said, "I have set before you life and death, blessing and curses. Now choose life."

Then Moses called Joshua before him and "in the presence of all Israel" Moses passed the leadership over to him. Bravely, but perhaps with tears in his eyes, Moses said to Joshua, "Be strong and courageous, for you must go with this people into the land that the Lord swore to their forefathers to give them. . . . The Lord himself goes before you and will be with you; he will never leave you nor forsake you. Do not be afraid; do not be discouraged."

Moses and Joshua went together into the tabernacle and

"the Lord appeared at the Tent in a pillar of cloud." God's presence showed the people that the choice of Joshua as their new leader was God's choice, too.

When the meeting was over, the people streamed back to their tents. Some were weeping; others were talking about Joshua and the kind of leader he would make; the children were playing as though nothing important had happened.

Silence settled down over the camp. Everybody turned in for the night—all except one.

Slowly through the darkening twilight moved the figure of a lonely old man. His work was done. His last command had been given. His last farewell had been said. Now he climbed Mount Nebo to "the top of Pisgah" to meet the One he had served so faithfully and so long.

This time no Aaron went with him, no Eleazar, no Joshua. On his last journey he walked alone.

With the dawn, he looked down upon the camp of the people whom he had loved so much. Then his eyes roamed across the Jordan valley, westward, northward, southward. There it was! The beautiful land! The goodly land! For a moment it was all spread out before him in one glorious panorama. How wonderful! How well worth all the struggle, the toil, the waiting!

It was the last thing he saw on earth. Then the old eyes closed. Moses fell asleep in the arms of God.

"So Moses the servant of the Lord died there in the land of Moab. . . . And he buried him" (Deuteronomy 34:5, 6, KJV).

73

From the top of Pisgah, Moses took a long look at the fruitful valleys and grassy plains of the Promised Land, which Israel was now to inherit after their wilderness wanderings.

The Scarlet Cord

(Deuteronomy 34:5-12; Joshua 1:1-2:21)

JOSHUA waited in the camp, wondering when Moses would return. But he never came back. Perhaps Joshua sent out search parties to look for him, but if so, they never found him. He had just disappeared.

Then the Lord Himself broke the sad news. "Moses my servant is dead." So "the Israelites grieved for Moses . . . thirty days." Everyone was sad to think that the grand old man was gone. For a while there was a feeling of emptiness and loneliness in every heart. But they could not mourn forever. There was work to be done. They must prepare for the great invasion.

God told Joshua, "Get ready to cross the Jordan River. . . . As I was with Moses, so I will be with you; I will never leave you nor forsake you. Be strong and courageous."

Joshua needed courage at this moment. The whole burden of leadership had just fallen on him. He had the job of planning for the future, and he couldn't go to Moses for advice. From now on, he had to make all the decisions himself.

He might have been a little worried as he thought of all he

74

had to do, and this may be why God said to him again and again, "Be strong and very courageous."

The first thing Joshua did on his own was to send two men across the river Jordan to find out about the defenses of Jericho and learn anything else that might be helpful in planning the attack.

These two spies crossed the river, and by mixing with the people going in and out of the city, managed to get inside without any trouble. Then, climbing to the top of the wall, they found a house where they decided to rent a room for the night.

Thinking they were safe, they talked with Rahab, the owner of the house, and found out many interesting things. Suddenly, however, they heard the clank of arms outside.

"The soldiers!" cried Rahab. "To the roof!"

The two spies fled upstairs as fast as they could go, and Rahab followed them. On the roof were stalks of flax, which Rahab quickly piled on top of them. Then she hurried down to the door where the soldiers were already knocking loudly.

"In the king's name," they cried as she opened the door, "bring out the men who came to you, . . . because they have come to spy out the whole land."

Rahab said she didn't know where the men came from or where they had gone. "Go after them quickly," she said. "You may catch up with them." The soldiers left without searching the house. They hurried to the Jordan, feeling sure the spies must have gone that way.

Meanwhile, Rahab went back to the roof. She removed the stalks of flax covering the two men and talked to them again.

"I know that the Lord has given this land to you," she said, "and that . . . all who live in this country are melting in fear because of you. We have heard how the Lord dried up the water of the Red Sea for you when you came out of Egypt, and what you did to Sihon and Og, the two kings of the Amorites east of the Jordan. . . . When we heard of it, our hearts melted and everyone's courage failed because of you."

Rahab was sure the children of Israel would enjoy the same success when they crossed the Jordan, because, she told them, "Your God is God in heaven above and on the earth below." So she asked the two men to make a bargain with her. She would help them escape if they would promise that she and all her relatives would be spared when Israel captured Jericho. The spies agreed.

Late that night, Rahab let the men down over the wall with a rope. When they were ready to slip away into the darkness, they whispered to her as loudly as they dared, "When we come back, tie this scarlet cord in the window, and make sure all your family is in your house." The cord would tell the soldiers of Israel which house to spare.

As soon as the spies were gone, Rahab tied the scarlet cord in the window of the house, where it remained for many days. Whenever Rahab looked at it, she told herself, *That will keep me safe.* She was so sure of it that she persuaded her father and mother and all her brothers and sisters to come and stay in her house.

They believed her story and began to trust in the scarlet cord too. And how glad they were for that cord later on when the city fell to the Israelites! Everyone in that house was saved.

It was just like when the Israelites sprinkled the blood of the lamb on the doorposts of their homes in Egypt the night the firstborn were killed. Every home with the blood was spared. It will be just like that in the future. Every heart that has the blood of Christ on its doorposts, or the scarlet cord of His love in the window, will be spared in the day of judgment. 🖋

← PAINTING BY FRED COLLINS

The two soldiers sent by Joshua to spy on Jericho found refuge in Rahab's home, and she helped them escape under cover of darkness on a red cord she hung from her window.

Crossing the Jordan

(Joshua 2:22-4:24)

THE TWO spies hid in the hills near Jericho for three days, until they were sure the soldiers looking for them had gone home. Then they made their way back across the river Jordan to the camp of Israel.

Joshua was waiting for them. "The people are all afraid of us," they told him, remembering what Rahab had said.

Calling his officers, Joshua explained what the spies had found and that it was time to take Jericho. Then he told them to go through the camp and tell everyone to prepare food and be ready to move in three days.

You can imagine the excitement as the people heard the news. They had been waiting so long for this moment! Only three days more and they would be in Canaan. Next Sabbath they would be in the land of milk and honey. It sounded too good to be true.

There was just one problem—the river Jordan. It was "at flood stage all during harvest," overflowing its banks. How did Joshua plan to take thousands of people across it? Was he going to build a bridge or boats—or what?

The three days went by quickly. Everybody was happy and busy preparing food, folding tents, packing bedding, and loading wagons. But no one saw any sign of work being done on a bridge or a boat.

Word went through the camp that everyone was to watch the Levites for the signal to start. "When you see the ark of the covenant of the Lord your God, and the priests, who are Levites, carrying it," said Joshua, "you are to move out from your positions and follow it."

Everyone looked toward the center of the camp, where the tabernacle had been standing for the past few weeks. It was no longer there. Already the gold-plated woodwork had been taken apart, the beautiful curtains carefully folded, and the articles of furniture reverently covered.

But still there was the Jordan, so wide and swift and deep. What *was* Joshua going to do about the Jordan?

The day before the march was to begin, he said to the

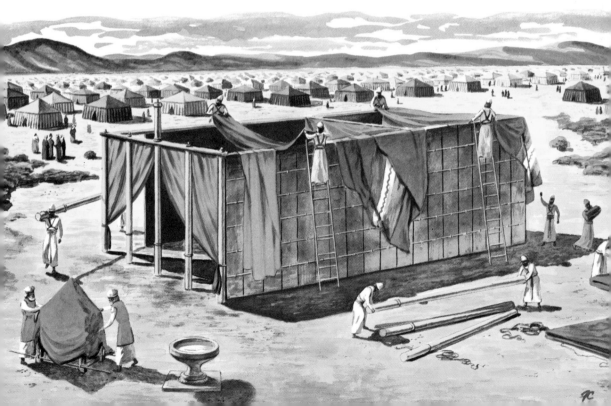

people, "Consecrate yourselves, for tomorrow the Lord will do amazing things among you." This created more excitement. The Lord had worked wonders for them before. What would He do now?

That last night was a night of prayer. Fathers and mothers, boys and girls, gave themselves to God again, and asked forgiveness for their sins. They wanted to be ready when He drew near.

Early the next morning Joshua called the people together and said to them, "Come here and listen to the words of the Lord your God. This is how you will know that the living God is among you. . . . See, the ark of the covenant of the Lord of all the earth will go into the Jordan ahead of you. . . . And as soon as the priests who carry the ark of the Lord—the Lord of all the earth—set foot in the Jordan, its waters flowing downstream will be cut off and stand up in a heap."

A thrill swept through the waiting people. "Are we going to cross the Jordan on dry land as our fathers passed through the Red Sea?" they asked one another.

The priests carrying the ark moved down the slope toward

the river. All held their breath. Thousands of boys and girls stood on tiptoe to get a good view, wondering what was going to happen.

Nearer and nearer the priests came to the water's edge. Still the river rolled majestically by.

Nearer and nearer. Suppose nothing happened? Would they just go on walking right into the water? Or would Joshua tell them to stop?

Nearer and nearer. Just a few steps more. Five, four, three, two, one.

Look! Their feet touched the water!

Suddenly something happened. Nobody knew what. They just could see that the water was 10 feet away. Twenty feet. Thirty feet. A hundred feet. Now there was dry land all the way

across. To the right, to the left, there was no sign of water. Somehow, somewhere, miraculously, the river had been dammed up and had stopped flowing.

The priests moved on. At Joshua's orders they stood still in the middle of the river bed, in the place of greatest danger if the water began to flow again. Seeing them there, the people began to cross. By thousands and tens of thousands they hurried from one side to the other, driving their wagons and their cattle as fast as they would go. It must have been an amazing sight!

The people of Jericho, watching from the walls of their city, were struck dumb with fear. They had never seen anything like this.

Hour after hour the Israelites continued to cross until the last man, the last woman, the last little boy, and the last little girl were safely on the other side.

Joshua sent word to the priests holding the ark in the middle of the river bed to "come up out of the Jordan."

They came, and were they glad! Hardly had they reached the bank when the people heard a dull roar somewhere in the distance and the pent-up waters came flooding all over the place where the priests had just been standing.

Everybody stared at the water in amazement. It was hard to believe. The river was in full flood as it had been before! Yet thousands of people had crossed from one side to the other without bridge or boat! So *this* was the wonder

God had promised to perform!

To make sure the people would never forget this marvelous miracle, Joshua had told 12 men, one from each tribe, to carry 12 big rocks out of the middle of the river bed. Now he had them piled in a heap as a memorial of the great event. "In the future when your descendants ask their fathers, 'What do these stones mean?' tell them, 'Israel crossed the Jordan on dry ground. For the Lord your God dried up the Jordan before you.' " "He did this so that all the peoples of the earth might know that the hand of the Lord is powerful and so that you might always fear the Lord your God."

Unfortunately, the heap of stones disappeared with the years. So did the memory of what God had done. ✒

The Captain Appears

(Joshua 5:10-6:5)

SAFELY across the river Jordan, the children of Israel pitched their tents with a joy in their hearts they had never known before. They were in Canaan at last! Their feet stood on the Promised Land.

With deep thankfulness to God, they kept the Passover. This celebration reminded them of the deliverance from Egypt 40 years before. Somehow it seemed to fit in wonderfully with the way God had just led them through the Jordan.

The next morning they ate food that they found in Canaan, and the morning after that, no more manna fell. The Bible says "the manna stopped the day after they ate this food from the land." No doubt a few people, from habit, went out to gather some for breakfast, but there wasn't any. They never saw the manna again. It was another sign that a new life, a new day, had begun for them.

One day, perhaps as evening was falling on the Jordan valley and the camp of Israel was growing quiet, Joshua went off by himself to pray. He was troubled. Better than anyone else,

85

← PAINTING BY HARRY ANDERSON

Before trying to take Jericho Joshua went out of the camp to pray. He did not know he would meet the Captain of the Lord's host, who had come to give him help from heaven.

he knew the difficulties ahead. Not far away was Jericho, so near that he could even see the soldiers on the walls. He wondered how such a city, so strong, so well defended, could be taken by people who knew so little about fighting. Beyond Jericho were a hundred other cities just like it, full of fierce, cruel people who would fight to the death to keep Israel from taking them.

Then there were those mountains he could see in the twilight, so high and steep, barring his way to the sea. How could he take thousands of people over them?

Joshua told God how helpless he felt and asked for wisdom so that he would know what to do.

Suddenly, as Joshua raised his head, he saw Someone standing nearby—a man with a sword in His hand. Joshua's hand must have felt for his own sword as he stepped toward the stranger. "Friend or foe?" he asked, as any soldier would. "Are you for us or for our enemies?"

"Neither," said the Stranger, "but as commander of the army of the Lord I have now come."

The commander of the army! thought Joshua. Wasn't *he* the commander? Then the truth dawned upon him. This must be the Lord Himself, the real Commander of Israel. He had come to give him the help, the wisdom, the courage, for which he had prayed.

"Then Joshua fell facedown to the ground in reverence, and asked him, 'What message does my Lord have for his servant?' "

The Lord had much to say to him, but first He reminded

THE CAPTAIN APPEARS

Joshua to be reverent in God's presence. He told Joshua to remove his sandals because the place on which he was standing was holy ground, just as He had reminded Moses at the burning bush. "And Joshua did so."

Then the Lord told him what he had wanted to know the most—how to capture Jericho. Israel was not to fight at all, but just to walk around and around the city. Then everyone was to give a big shout, and the walls would fall down. It would be just as easy as that.

How simple the problem seemed to Joshua now! There was no need for him to worry anymore. The Commander of the army was in charge, and He was sure to win the victory.

All our problems will become simple if we let the Lord take full charge of our lives.

The Shout That Wrecked a City

(Joshua 6:6-20)

THE WATCHMEN on the walls of Jericho were puzzled. Ever since they had seen the children of Israel cross the dry bed of the river, they had been expecting an attack. But none had come.

The gates of the city were closed. Every able-bodied man was fully armed, ready for action at a moment's notice. Archers were posted on the walls to shoot down any attacker. But none came.

Spies reported that the Israelites were going through certain religious ceremonies, but had no big engines of war for dealing with walled cities. Nor were they building any. It all seemed so strange. Were they planning just to sit there and starve them out?

Then one day the watchmen in Jericho saw a procession forming outside the camp of Israel.

"This must be it," they said to one another, and soldiers were ordered to their positions. But still the attack did not come.

Instead, they saw thousands of armed men begin to march not *toward* the city, but *around* it. Following them was a group of priests carrying the strange object they had seen in the middle of the Jordan river when the Israelites had crossed it. Then came more armed men. The procession marched on and on until it had gone completely around the city. Then it went back into the camp of Israel and dispersed.

"That's a funny way to attack a city!" said someone on the walls. "If that's how they mean to make war on us, we won't have much to worry about."

"I don't like it," said another. "Did you notice how quiet they were? No one said a word as far as I could hear."

The next day the same thing happened—the same procession, the same silent march around the city. It was so strange.

It was the same the next day, and the next, for six days in a row.

"What are they up to?" many people in the city began to ask. "Do they think they're going to frighten us by just walking

89

around and around like this?"

Then came the seventh day. Early in the morning, the procession started again. At first there seemed to be no difference. And there wasn't—until one complete circuit had been made. Then, instead of going back to camp as usual, the soldiers and the priests walked around the city again. Then again and again. Four times, five times, six times.

Still not a spear was thrown, not an arrow was shot. And still there was no sound except the noise of the priests' trumpets and the tramp, tramp, tramp of the marching people.

No doubt the walls were thronged with onlookers by now, all watching the amazing sight. All wondered what it meant and what might happen next. The procession marched around the city for the seventh time.

Suddenly, as the priests blew on their trumpets once more, there was a mighty shout. It was so loud that it seemed as if every soldier in the ranks of the Israelites had shouted at exactly the same moment. The sound wave appeared to strike the walls like a battering ram, for at that precise moment there was a shuddering and a shaking as if an earthquake had hit the city. The great walls began to crumble and fall. Hundreds of the defenders and spectators were tossed to the ground and killed, leaving the city wide open to the Israelites.

Soon, the fighting was all over. Jericho had been captured. Israel's first victory in Canaan had been won. 🖋

PAINTING BY FRED COLLINS

Buried Sin

(Joshua 7)

A S THE Israelites returned to camp after the capture of Jericho, they felt very pleased with themselves. They had taken the most important city in the Jordan valley without a fight! It was amazing. They began to think that if all the cities of Canaan could be captured as easily as this, they would possess the land in no time.

Thinking thoughts like these, they set out to take the city of Ai. Because it was much smaller than Jericho, some of the leaders said it would not be necessary for all the men of Israel to go against it. "Send two or three thousand men to take it," they told Joshua, "and do not weary all the people."

So about 3,000 men went up to attack Ai, and were defeated. Thirty-six men were killed, and the rest came home feeling very discouraged.

Something had gone wrong. Joshua felt almost as bad as the rest. He couldn't understand it. Where was the Commander of the Lord's army who had promised victory?

"Then Joshua tore his clothes and fell facedown to the

ground before the ark of the Lord, remaining there till evening. The elders of Israel did the same, and sprinkled dust on their heads."

This was a strange position for the would-be conqueror of a country, and the Lord didn't like it. "Stand up!" He said to Joshua; "What are you doing down on your face?"

Then the Lord told him what was the matter. Someone in the camp had committed a very serious sin. God had said that "all the silver and gold and the articles of bronze and iron are sacred to the Lord and must go into his treasury." "Israel," He continued, "you have in your possession some things I ordered you to destroy. You cannot stand against your enemies until you get rid of these things" (TEV).

Someone had disobeyed orders and kept part of the riches of Jericho for himself. But how could Joshua find the person who had stolen what belonged to God? Then the Lord told him to draw lots, first to find the tribe to which the man belonged, then to find his family, and finally to find the man himself.

Meanwhile, Achan, who had stolen the items and buried them in his tent, felt perfectly safe. *They'll never catch me,* he told himself. *Never.*

Even when Joshua called all the people together and

began to draw lots, Achan did not feel worried. How could they ever find him among so many, many thousands of people—especially when no one in the camp knew what he had done?

But when he heard that out of the 12 tribes the tribe of Judah had been chosen, he became a little anxious. *That's my tribe,* he told himself. *But think of all the thousands of families in Judah. I'm still all right.*

He became more worried when he learned that when lots were cast among the families of Judah, the family of the Zerahites had been chosen. *That's my family,* he said. *I don't like this. It's getting too close.*

Minutes later the search came closer still, for Zimri, Achan's grandfather, was chosen. As the old man went forward to speak with Joshua, Achan's face turned pale.

The priests began to cast lots on Zimri's children and grandchildren. Then Achan heard his own name called . . . and his heart sank. His dishonesty had been discovered, and he could hide it no longer.

"My son," said Joshua kindly but solemnly, "give glory to the Lord, the God of Israel, and give him the praise. Tell me what you have done; do not hide it from me."

Trembling, Achan confessed. There was nothing else he could do. Yes, he was the one who had sinned. When Jericho was captured he had seen "a beautiful robe from Babylonia," which he thought would be nice to wear some day, and about five pounds of silver and about one and a quarter pounds of gold. "I coveted them and took them," he

94

said. "They are hidden in the ground inside my tent, with the silver underneath."

Joshua sent men to Achan's tent, and they soon found the stolen goods and brought them back. The items made a sad little pile in front of Joshua and the elders of Israel. The Babylonian robe didn't look nearly as beautiful as before. What a shame that Israel had suffered defeat in battle and many good men had been killed, because of this flimsy piece of cloth and a few bits of silver and gold!

Achan was sorry, terribly sorry. But it was too late to be sorry. He had to be punished. And he was.

He was taken to a valley where there were many stones, and the people threw stones at him until he died. "Over Achan they heaped up a large pile of rocks, which remains to this day."

The place was called Achor, meaning "trouble." And what a lot of trouble had been caused by that one little sin, a buried sin that wouldn't stay covered!

Moldy Bread

(*Joshua 8:1-29; 9*)

AFTER Achan had been punished, Ai was easily captured. Not with 3,000 men, though. All the people of war went up against it—just as they had against Jericho—and the city was destroyed.

As news of this second great victory spread through the land, the people of Canaan became very frightened. Some of the rulers of the larger cities decided to band together and make war on Israel. Others thought it would be better to make a treaty of peace with the invaders if they could. Among these were the leading men of Gibeon, who thought up quite a bright idea to save themselves.

Their city was not very far from Ai, and they guessed that if they did not do something soon, it might be their turn to be destroyed next. So they dressed themselves up as a delegation from a distant country, "whose donkeys were loaded with worn-out sacks and old wineskins, cracked and mended. The men put worn and patched sandals on their feet and wore old clothes. All the bread . . . was dry and moldy. Then they went to Joshua in the camp at Gilgal and said to him and the men of Israel, 'We have come from a distant country; make a treaty with us.' "

Some of the leaders of Israel were a bit suspicious of the travel-stained strangers. They looked over these visitors very carefully, but no one detected the fraud. So Joshua asked them who they were and where they had come from.

Wearily they answered, "Your servants have come from a very distant country because of the fame of the Lord your God. For we have heard reports of him: all that he did in Egypt, and all that he did to the two kings of the Amorites east of the Jordan—Sihon king of Heshbon, and Og king of Bashan."

They carefully avoided mentioning Jericho and Ai, which would have given them away. Then, seeing that their speech had made a big impression on Joshua and the princes of Israel, they went on to point to the food they had brought with them. "This bread of ours," they said sadly, "was warm when we packed it at home on the day we left to come to you. But now see how dry and moldy it is. And these wineskins that we filled were new, but see how cracked they are. And our clothes and sandals are worn out by the very long journey."

How they kept their faces straight while they told all

these lies, I can't imagine. But they did. And Joshua believed them. So did the other leaders who listened to them. That moldy bread seemed to prove that what the travelers were saying was true. "Then Joshua made a treaty of peace with them to let them live, and the leaders of the assembly ratified it by oath."

Of course, it wasn't long before the fraud was discovered. In fact, within three days the truth was out. You can imagine how foolish and angry Joshua and the others felt about it. But they kept their word. When they came to Gibeon, they left it unharmed. However, as a punishment for their lies, the Gibeonites were told that they had to be "woodcutters and water carriers" for the children of Israel forever.

Why were Joshua and the princes of Israel deceived by these people? The Bible says, "The men of Israel sampled their provisions but did not inquire of the Lord."

God was ready to tell them what to do about this matter, just as He had told them how to take Jericho and Ai. But perhaps they were feeling so proud of themselves over their two great victories that they had thought it wasn't necessary to ask God about such a little matter as this. So they were deceived by a piece of moldy bread.

It's a good thing to take every question to God and let Him guide in every detail of our lives.

The Sun Stands Still

(Joshua 10-21)

THAT piece of moldy bread the Gibeonites showed to Joshua brought him more trouble than he expected.

Not long after he had signed the treaty with them, they sent him an urgent message asking for help. They were about to be attacked by five kings of nearby cities, and would he please come at once? "Come up to us quickly and save us! Help us," they pleaded, "because all the Amorite kings from the hill country have joined forces against us."

These five kings had planned to attack the Israelites and stop their invasion of Canaan. Naturally, when they heard that the Gibeonites had made peace with Israel, they were very angry. Traitors, they called them, and set out to punish them. That's when the Gibeonites appealed to Joshua for help.

This time Joshua did not forget to ask God what to do. To his surprise, the Lord told him to go and help these people who had deceived him—and to go right away.

By marching all night, the armies of Israel reached Gibeon just in time. Taken by surprise, the soldiers of the five kings scattered in all directions.

During the fighting that followed, two amazing things happened. First, a sudden hail storm beat down the enemy so badly that "more of them died from the hailstones than were killed by the swords of the Israelites."

Then, as the chase continued toward evening and Joshua saw that many enemy soldiers would escape in the darkness, he prayed for more time to finish the job.

Joshua realized that this was a very important battle. If he won it, he would break the power of the Canaanites once and for all. His path to the sea would be open, and to all Canaan too. He *must* win it. Oh, for more daylight! If only the sun would not go down!

Suddenly Joshua looked toward the setting sun and cried, "O sun, stand still over Gibeon, O moon, over the Valley of Aijalon."

Just how it happened, I do not know. But the Bible says that "the sun stood still, and the moon stopped" until the battle was won.

Hour after hour, when normally there would have been darkness, there was light. The sun continued to shine. In fact, the sun "delayed going down about a whole day." It just stayed where it was in the sky. "There has never been a day like it before or since, a day when the Lord listened to a man. Surely the Lord was fighting for Israel!"

Of course, everyone in Palestine knew about this and marveled at the long, long day. And when they heard that it had happened just so Israel could defeat the five kings, they

didn't have much fight left in them. Israel won victory after victory in the battles that followed. "So Joshua took the entire land, just as the Lord had directed Moses."

At last, when all the fighting was over, Joshua carefully divided the land among the people of Israel. To make sure everyone would be satisfied, he set up a committee of 21 men who explored the whole country and "wrote its description on a scroll, town by town, in seven parts." With this scroll beside him, he cast lots for the land, and the various tribes accepted the portions that came to them. Then they all set off to start their new life in the Promised Land.

"Not one of all the Lord's good promises to the house of Israel failed; every one was fulfilled."

Joshua's Last Days

(Joshua 14:6-15; 19:49, 50; 23; 24:1-31)

WHEN the land of Canaan was being divided among the tribes of Israel, two beautiful things happened.

The first was when old Caleb came to make a request. What do you suppose this 85-year-old veteran asked for? A nice, flat piece of fertile land by the Jordan? No, indeed. Not he. "Give me this hill country," he said, pointing to the land where the giant sons of Anak still lived. "The Lord helping me, I will drive them out just as he said."

It was these very sons of Anak who had frightened the people nearly 40 years earlier. Now Caleb, brave to the last, offered to meet them in battle himself. He did, and he won.

Then, when the dividing of the land was almost over, Joshua's turn came. What did he ask for? As a leader, he might have demanded a very large, beautiful tract of land, but he didn't. Instead, he asked for one little ruined city, which he had to rebuild. When it was given to him, he called it Timnath Serah, meaning "the portion that remains." This was the mark of a truly great man. He took nothing for himself until everyone else had been cared for.

Years passed by. Years of peace and joy for Israel. Joshua celebrated his hundredth birthday. Soon after this, feeling that his end was near, he called all the people together as Moses had done just before he died.

When they came to him, he reminded them again of all God's goodness to them from the day God had called Abraham out of Ur of the Chaldeans. Carrying their minds back to the days of their slavery in Egypt, he spoke of the great deliverance at the Red Sea, of the miraculous crossing of the Jordan, and of all the wonderful victories God had given them since they had entered Canaan.

"So be very careful to love the Lord your God," he begged them. "Now fear the Lord and serve him with all faithfulness."

Then he warned them of what would happen if they ever forgot the God who had blessed them so, adding those last wonderful words of his: "Choose for yourselves this day whom you will serve. . . . As for me and my household, we will serve the Lord."

Deeply touched by their old leader's faith and his deep concern for them, the people replied, "We will serve the Lord our God and obey him."

They meant it. I'm sure they did. And as long as Joshua lived, they kept their word.

Joshua died "at the age of a hundred and ten." And where do you suppose they buried him? In his own little city of Tim-nath Serah, "the portion that remains"—a fitting place for one whose name will remain forever.

PART THREE

Stories of

the Days of the Judges

(Judges 1:1-Ruth 4:22)

SEA OF GALILEE

BALAAM MET BY THE ANGEL

VALLED CITIES OF THE CANAANITES

BAAL WORSHIP

MT. EBAL

MT. GERIZIM

TABERNACLE AT SHILOH

RIVER JABBOK

TENT CITIES

LAND OF GIANTS

CROSSING THE JORDAN

THE FALL OF JERICHO

RIVER ARNON

DEAD SEA

GIBEONITES

SETTLEMENT OF CANAAN
UNDER JOSHUA'S LEADERSHIP

The Place of Weepers

(Judges 1:1-2:15)

WHEN the tribes of Israel were given the land of Canaan, it was with the understanding that they were to drive out the rest of the wicked people they found there. They were to smash their idols, break down their altars, and create a pure and holy nation in Palestine that would glow with the glory of God in an evil world. But they didn't do it. They got tired too soon.

Eager to build homes for themselves and begin farming again, they found all sorts of excuses for not doing exactly what God, through Joshua, had told them to do.

The tribe of Judah, we read, "took possession of the hill country, but they were unable to drive the people from the plains, because they had iron chariots." What did iron chariots have to do with it? Couldn't God have found a way to deal with that problem, as He had dealt with so many problems before?

The first chapter of Judges is one long story of failure.

"But Manasseh did not drive out the people of Beth Shan."

"Nor did Ephraim drive out the Canaanites living in Gezer."

"Neither did Zebulun drive out the Canaanites living in Kitron."

And so on and so on. Then it says, "The Amorites confined the Danites to the hill country, not allowing them to come down into the plain." What a shameful thing to happen after all the smashing victories Israel had had under Joshua! It was all very disappointing.

What God thought about it is revealed in the words of "the angel of the Lord" who came to speak to the children of Israel at a place called Bokim.

"I brought you up out of Egypt," he said sadly, "and led you into the land that I swore to give to your forefathers. I said, 'I will never break my covenant with you, and you shall not make a covenant with the people of this land, but you shall break down their altars.' Yet you have disobeyed me. Why have you done this?"

Then He reminded them of the warning He had given them through Moses long before: "Now therefore I tell you that I will not drive them out before you; they will be thorns in your sides and their gods will be a snare to you."

As the children of Israel listened to these solemn words of rebuke and warning, they became very sad. They knew that this messenger from heaven was telling the truth. They had failed to

do as God had told them. They hadn't driven out the Canaanites. They hadn't destroyed their idols. They hadn't broken
down their altars. They had been lazy, selfish, and disobedient.
And now God wasn't going to help them anymore.

First one began to cry, then another and another, until
everyone was in tears. "The people wept aloud, and they called
that place Bokim," which means "place of weepers."

It was good that they wept. God was pleased to see that
they were sorry for their sins. The pity is that their repentance
didn't last very long. All too soon they again "did evil in the
eyes of the Lord and served the Baals. They forsook the Lord,
the God of their fathers, who had brought them out of Egypt.
They followed and worshiped various gods."

"In his anger against Israel the Lord handed them over to
raiders who plundered them. He sold them to their enemies all
around, . . . Whenever Israel went out to fight, the hand of the
Lord was against them to defeat them, just as he had sworn to
them. They were in great distress."

Sad, sad day!

It is hard to think that people who had seen the Lord do so
many wonderful things for them could forget Him so quickly.
But they did. And what a price they had to pay! Before long
every city they had built, every home they lived in, became a
Bokim, a "place of weepers."

What a lesson for us all! May we never forget the Lord!

109

Seesaw Days

(Judges 2:11-6:1)

F OR MANY years after the death of Joshua, Israel's prosperity was like a seesaw. Sometimes it was up, sometimes it was down.

When the people forgot God and worshiped the idols of Canaan, they found themselves in big trouble. When they turned back to God, good times came again.

It was just like that—seesaw, seesaw. And what a pity! For God had planned such a wonderful time for them. He wanted them always to "ride on the heights of the land."* He wanted them to be the greatest, noblest nation that ever was, telling all the world about His love. But "they forsook him and served Baal," and so they had to go through terrible trouble.

"Then," the Bible says, "the Lord raised up judges, who saved them out of the hands of these raiders." But after each judge died, "the people returned to ways even more corrupt than those of their fathers, following other gods and serving and worshiping them. They refused to give up their evil practices and stubborn ways."

110

SEESAW DAYS

That was the story—seesaw, seesaw, down and up. The people turned away from God into trouble and turned from trouble back to God.

The first punishment came when God allowed the king of Mesopotamia to invade the country. For eight long years he controlled Israel. At last, when they were sorry for their sins and cried to God for deliverance, He helped Othniel, Caleb's nephew, drive out the invader. With his uncle's brave spirit, Othniel rallied the people and led them to victory.

Everything went well for another 40 years, but after Othniel died, the people forgot God again and "did evil in the eyes of the Lord." So He let Eglon, king of Moab, take the country, and Israel spent 18 years under another foreign king.

Eventually the people were sorry they had done wrong, and the Lord forgave them. This time He sent a man called

Ehud to rescue them. He won a great victory over Moab, and there was peace for 80 years. "After Ehud died, the Israelites once again did evil in the eyes of the Lord. So the Lord sold them into the hands of Jabin, a king of Canaan."

They were just like some little children I know. So naughty that they had to be spanked. Then sorry for their sins. Then good for a little while. Then naughty all over again. Maybe you know someone like that.

It was too bad, because not only was God's beautiful purpose spoiled, but everyone was so miserable and poor. The invaders stole their crops and their money and made them work for nothing.

When King Jabin took over the Israelites' country, Sisera was the commander of his army. He had 900 iron chariots and "cruelly oppressed the Israelites." That must have been a very bad time. But when the people were sorry for their sins again, the Lord sent Deborah to help them.

Deborah was "a mother in Israel" and a prophetess. She encouraged all Israel to go and fight Sisera, in spite of all his iron chariots. Led by this very brave woman, Israel won a great victory. Another woman, Jael, killed Sisera while he was asleep.

"Praise the Lord," sang Deborah after the battle. And the people did praise Him. They were so glad to be free again. "So may all your enemies perish, O Lord!" they cried. "But may they who love you be like the sun when it rises in its strength."

For a while it seemed as if a great revival was about to sweep over the people. The watching angels must have thought that perhaps the people of Israel had learned their lesson at last. Maybe God would be able to bless them from now on, as He so much wanted to do. But no, what looked like sunrise became sunset all too soon. Once again "the Israelites did evil in the eyes of the Lord, and for seven years he gave them into the hands of the Midianites."

How sad to see how easily a whole nation turned away from God. We need to pray that we will never do the same.

---

* Deuteronomy 32:13.

An Angel Burns the Dinner

(Judges 6:1-24)

AFTER seven years under the rule of the Midianites, things became so bad for the people of Israel that they fled from their homes and lived in dens and caves in the mountains. When some of the bravest men managed to plant their fields, enemy soldiers would destroy the crops before they were full grown. The Midianites "did not spare a living thing for Israel, neither sheep nor cattle nor donkeys." Everyone was starving.

The worst days in the desert were never as bad as these. How the poor Israelites must have longed for Moses and Joshua! It seemed as if God had left them forever. But He hadn't. In fact, He could bear Israel's misery no longer. He was always looking for the first sign that they were sorry for their sins, and He was always looking for someone He could use to deliver them.

This time He found a man in a little place called Ophrah. Here on a hot summer afternoon, a young man was threshing wheat by the wine press "to keep it from the Midianites." Since it wasn't time for the grape harvest, he thought they wouldn't

← PAINTING BY KREIGH COLLINS

When God needed a brave leader on whom He could depend to deliver the Israelites from the Midianites, He sent an angel to call Gideon, who was threshing wheat at Ophrah.

be looking around the wine press for a while.

Though he was tall, strong, and good looking, with the bearing of a prince, this young man's heart was sad as he thought of the evil times his people were facing. It seemed as if life was hardly worth living.

Suddenly, looking up from his work, he was startled to see a stranger sitting under a nearby oak. He had been sure that he was alone, hidden from all prying eyes. But no. Someone was looking at him. Who could it be? A Midianite?

The stranger spoke. "The Lord is with you, mighty warrior."

So! Then he must be a friend.

"But sir," said Gideon, pouring out everything that had been troubling him, "if the Lord is with us, why has all this happened to us? Where are all his wonders that our fathers told us about when they said, 'Did not the Lord bring us up out of Egypt?' But now the Lord has abandoned us and put us into the hand of Midian."

The stranger looked straight at him, right into his eyes, and said, "Go in the strength you have and save Israel out of Midian's hand."

"I?" said Gideon, with the same humility that Moses had shown when God called him at the burning bush. " 'But Lord,' Gideon asked, 'how can I save Israel? My clan is the weakest in Manasseh, and I am the least in my family.'

"The Lord answered, 'I will be with you, and you will strike down all the Midianites together.' "

Gideon could hardly believe his ears. He wondered if he

116

was dreaming. "Show me a sign that you are really talking with me," he said to the stranger. Then he remembered that the stranger was his guest, so Gideon asked him to wait while he went to get some food.

All excited, Gideon ran to his humble home. He cooked some meat, boiled some broth, and baked some fresh unleavened bread—all very scarce and precious foods when everyone was having such a hard time finding enough to eat. Then he hurried back to the oak, wondering whether his visitor would still be there.

He was. To Gideon's surprise, his visitor told him to put the meat and the bread on a nearby rock and pour out the broth.

Gideon did as he was told, though it must have seemed like a dreadful waste. The stranger touched the food with the end of

117

the staff that was in his hand, and "fire flared from the rock, consuming the meat and the bread." Then he vanished.

Now Gideon was sure his visitor had been an angel of the Lord. Bowing his head he cried, "Ah, Sovereign Lord! I have seen the angel of the Lord face to face!"

"Peace! Do not be afraid," the Lord whispered to him. "You are not going to die."

Deeply moved, Gideon's first thought was to build an altar to the God of heaven, the God of Abraham, Isaac, and Jacob, who had spoken to him in this place. So he piled stones on the rock where the fire had blazed, and called the place "Jehovah-shalom," meaning "The Lord is Peace."

That prayer was the longing of Gideon's heart. And the Lord wanted to send peace. But there were many things that needed to be done first.

The Wet-Dry Fleece

(Judges 6:25-40)

THAT very night the Lord spoke to Gideon again, telling him just what he was to do. God wanted him to begin his work right away, at home. The first step toward driving the Midianites out of the country was to tear down the altar of Baal in his own backyard.

So, in the middle of the night, taking 10 of his young friends to help him, Gideon broke down the altar of Baal that his father had built. Before sunrise it was in pieces, and the grove of trees around it was cut down.

Next he sent messengers through the country calling for volunteers to help him fight the Midianites. Thousands flocked to him.

But Gideon was still worried about his call. Had God really spoken to him? Would He stand by him in the battles ahead? He decided to ask God to show him very clearly that there had been no mistake.

Taking a wool fleece, he laid it on the ground. Then he said to God that if the dew fell only on the fleece, while the ground around it was dry, he would know that God really did want him to save Israel from the Midianites.

The next morning the fleece was so wet that Gideon wrung a bowlful of water out of it. The ground around it was dry.

But Gideon still wasn't quite sure. The fleece *might* have become damp from the moisture in the air. To make quite sure, he asked God to give him one more sign. Tomorrow morning, he said, "make the fleece dry and the ground covered with dew.

"That night God did so. Only the fleece was dry; all the ground was covered with dew."

As Gideon picked up the dry fleece from the wet ground, he knew for sure that God was directing him. I can see him standing there alone with his head bowed, saying, "Thank You, dear Lord. I'm ready now. I know everything will be all right."

Three Hundred Heroes

(Judges 7:1-8; 19-23)

MORE and more of the men of Israel found their way to the place where Gideon had raised the standard of revolt against the Midianites, until he had an army of 32,000.

"You have too many," said the Lord.

"Too many!" This would be hard for any army commander to understand.

"That's right," the Lord told him. "If this many people fight and win, they will think that they earned the victory themselves."

To everyone's surprise, Gideon said to the crowd of men around him, "Anyone who trembles with fear may turn back and leave."

To Gideon's dismay, he saw his army melt away. Twenty-two thousand men went home!

I imagine he said, "This is impossible. With only 10,000 men left, perhaps we had better give up the whole idea."

"But the Lord said to Gideon, 'There are still too many men.' "

Still too many! How could it be?

Then the Lord told him to take the 10,000 men he had left to a nearby stream, and He would point out which of them should go into battle.

When everyone had gathered at the water's edge, the Lord told Gideon that every man who went down on his knees to drink should be sent home. Only those who brought the water to their mouths with their hands and lapped it "like a dog" were to remain.

When it was all over, how many soldiers do you suppose Gideon had left? Just 300. And why were they chosen? Perhaps it was because they were so eager to fight they didn't even want to take the time to kneel down beside the stream to drink.

Now what was Gideon going to do? How could he hope to defeat the great army of Midianites with only a handful of soldiers, however brave and devoted they were?

When the Lord saw how worried Gideon was, He said to him, "With the three hundred men . . . I will save you."

122

And that's what happened. The Lord told Gideon to give each man a trumpet, a torch, and an empty pitcher. At the right moment the torch was to be lighted and hidden inside the pitcher.

Under the cover of darkness Gideon placed his men in three companies around the camp of the Midianites. Then in the middle of the night, at a signal from him, each man broke his pitcher, revealing the flaming torch. Then all blew their trumpets and shouted at the top of their voices, "A sword for the Lord and for Gideon!"

The sleeping Midianites woke up with a start. Seeing the torches and hearing loud shouts all around them, they were sure the Israelites were attacking them from all sides. Losing their heads, they struck out right and left, killing one another by the thousands. The rest fled. The 300 heroes chased them until everyone was exhausted but they kept up the chase until a decisive victory was won.

Gideon's victory was as great as any in Israel's history. It showed that God was still ready to help His people. He was still able to save them, whether he used a large army or a small one. 🖋

A Very Sad Story

(Judges 11:29-40)

W E DON'T know her name—only that she was the daughter of a man called Jephthah, who was "a mighty warrior" God used to help Israel after the death of Gideon. I am sure she loved her daddy very much, and I know he dearly loved her. The Bible says she was an only child. She must have been very lonesome for her daddy when he went away to fight, especially since she didn't have any brothers and sisters to play with.

Perhaps like most girls, she dreamed that when she was grown up, she would get married and have lots of boys and girls of her own. Maybe she hoped that would make up for being so lonesome as a child.

Later on, when she was a lovely young lady, her daddy went out to fight the Ammonites, who had threatened to take away much of Israel's land. He made a strange vow and promised the Lord that if he won the battle, he would give God the first thing that came out of his house to meet him on his return.

Of course, he expected that it would be one of the animals

which, in those days, for safety's sake, people kept in their houses. He thought it might be a lamb, or a kid, or a calf, which he would gladly offer up as a burnt offering.

After his victory over the Ammonites, Jephthah returned home. Imagine his feelings when he saw not an animal but his own precious daughter running to meet him!

At any other time he would have been overjoyed to see her. She looked so sweet and pretty as she came dancing down the hillside toward him with tambourines in her hands, singing for joy like any other girl who loved her daddy would have done.

But poor Jephthah was heartbroken. To his daughter's amazement, he burst into tears and tore his clothes, as people did in those days when they were very upset about something.

"What's the matter, Daddy?" I can hear her saying. "Aren't you glad to see me?"

Then he told her about the vow he had made, and how he never dreamed that she would be the one to come to meet him. I imagine they just cried and cried in each other's arms!

Of course, he couldn't offer up his daughter as a burnt offering, but he had to keep his promise to give her to the Lord. A promise made to God is very important. So he said she must never marry, but serve the Lord as a single girl all her life.

It was very hard for her to take. She had dearly wanted to have boys and girls of her own. Now she would never be able to have a family. Many girls might have become very bitter and angry about the whole thing, but she didn't.

" 'My Father,' she replied, 'you have given your word to the Lord. Do to me just as you promised, now that the Lord has avenged you of your enemies, the Ammonites. But grant me this one request. . . . Give me two months to roam the hills and weep with my friends, because I will never marry.' "

So she went up into the mountains to cry about it with some of her girl friends. Afterward, when she was home again, her father "did to her as he had vowed."

That's why I think this is such a very sad story.

The Much-wanted Boy

(Judges 13:2-24)

HIS MOTHER wanted him, his father wanted him, but most of all God wanted him.

Manoah and his wife had longed for a little boy, but no baby came. Then one day a messenger from God met the woman and told her that she would have a son. He also said that she must dedicate him to God from the day of his birth, because God had a great work for him to do. God wanted him to become a leader in Israel and save His people from the Philistines, who now ruled over them.

When she arrived home, the woman told her husband what had happened. "A man of God came to me," she said. "He looked like an angel of God, very awesome. I didn't ask him where he came from, and he didn't tell me his name. But he said to me, 'You will conceive and give birth to a son. Now then, drink no wine or other fermented drink and do not eat anything unclean, because the boy will be a Nazirite of God . . . until the day of his death.'"

Manoah didn't question his wife's story but he bowed in

prayer, saying, "O Lord, I beg you, let the man of God you sent to us come again to teach us how to bring up the boy who is to be born."

That was a very beautiful prayer, and the Lord heard it. The man of God came again and gave them both the same advice he had given before.

After they had talked together for a while about the baby, Manoah offered to bring the visitor a meal. But the stranger said he didn't want any food. However he said that if Manoah wanted to offer a sacrifice to God, that would be all right. So Manoah took the young goat that he was going to prepare for food and offered it as a burnt offering. Suddenly, as the fire rose around the sacrifice the man of God vanished, going up toward heaven in the flames.

Startled, "Manoah and his wife fell with their faces to the ground," sure that they had seen an angel of the Lord.

Manoah was afraid that both of them would die, but his wife was more sensible. No, she said, if the Lord had wanted to kill them both, He wouldn't have accepted their offering, and He wouldn't have sent an angel to tell them all about the baby.

She was right, and soon the baby boy arrived, just as the angel had said. Proudly and thankfully, they called him Samson. "He grew and the Lord blessed him."

How lovingly those two dear people watched over their little boy! How eagerly they looked forward to the day when he would be a grown man, ready to do the great work God wanted him to do!

But bitter disappointment lay ahead. 🍃

3-9

The Strongest Man
Who Ever Lived

(Judges 14-16)

SAMSON became the strongest man who ever lived. Thanks to the loving care his parents gave him, he grew to be so big and strong that nobody could overpower him. Once, when he was still quite young, he tore a lion apart with his bare hands.

But though his body was strong, he was selfish and headstrong and a great problem to his father and mother.

As Samson was growing up he fell in love with a Philistine girl and wanted to marry her right away. Naturally his parents tried to persuade him not to do such a thing. "Can't you find a nice Israelite girl to marry?" they said to him, kindly but earnestly. "Why do you want a wife from our enemies?"

But Samson wouldn't listen to them. "Get her for me," he said. "She's the right one for me." So he married her. And what a lot of trouble and sorrow that marriage brought to them all.

One day as Samson happened to pass the carcass of a lion he had killed, he noticed that there was a swarm of bees and honey in it. This gave him an idea for a bit of fun at his wedding feast. Thirty young men were at the wedding as guests, and he asked them the meaning of this riddle: "Out of the eater, something to eat; out of the strong, something sweet." Then he offered to give them each a suit of clothes if they could give the answer during the seven days of the feast. If they failed to answer in that time, they were to give him 30 suits.

Unable to guess the riddle the young men began to get worried. They were afraid they would all have to give their own clothes to Samson, and then what would they do?

On the seventh day they came to Samson's wife and persuaded her to try to find out the meaning of the riddle. She pleaded with Samson to tell her, and in a moment of weakness he did. Then she told the young men, and they came to Samson and said, "What is sweeter than honey? What is stronger than a lion?"

Samson was so angry that his wife had told his secret that he went and killed 30 Philistines and brought their clothes and gave them to the 30 young men. Then—after being with his wife only seven days—he left her in a huff and went back to his old home.

When he had cooled down a bit, he decided to go back to his wife, but he found that she had married someone else,

131

thinking he didn't love her anymore. This made Samson furious. To get even with the Philistines, he caught 300 foxes and tied them together in pairs, tail to tail, with a firebrand in between. Then he let the maddened animals loose in the grainfields and vineyards of the Philistines. You can imagine what happened. Those foxes must have set fire to hundreds of acres, leaving only blackened fields behind them.

Now it was the Philistines' turn to get angry. They marched into the land of Judah and demanded that Samson be handed over to them for punishment. So 3,000 men of Judah surrounded Samson, bound him, and gave him to the Philistines. But no sooner was he back among his enemies than he broke the ropes binding him as though they were "charred flax" and, picking up the jawbone of a donkey, slew a thousand men with it.

By this time Samson's fame as the strongest man on earth was spreading. Everybody was afraid of him. The Philistines couldn't catch him, however hard they tried. One night when he was in Gaza, the rulers of the city shut the gates so that he couldn't get away. But at midnight Samson carried away both gates and gateposts and dumped them on the top of a hill 38 miles (61 kilometers) away!

The next morning, when the Philistines saw that great gap in the walls of Gaza, they must have had a shock. But what could they do? This giant of a man was just too strong and too smart for them.

Then they heard that Samson had fallen in love with a woman named Delilah, and they made up their minds to work through her to get him. "Find the secret of his strength," they begged her. She tried to, but it wasn't easy. Three times Samson lied to her.

Once he told her that if she tied him up with seven fresh bowstrings, he would be helpless. But when she tied him up, he snapped them in a moment.

Another time he said that if she tied him with new strips of leather, he would be as weak as other men. But when she had gone to all the trouble of finding the leather and tying him up with them, he broke them as if they had been thread.

The third time he told her—for fun—that if she were to weave his hair in with the cloth she was making, he would never be able to get free. That night while he was asleep, she did that very thing. But in the morning he walked off with all the weaving machinery hanging from his head and laughed at her.

Day after day Delilah, pouting and fussing and teasing until "he was tired to death," asked Samson to tell her his secret. He just couldn't stand it any longer. Then he told her.

133

The secret of his strength, he said, lay in the fact that he was a Nazirite, a man dedicated to God. Because he was a Nazirite, his hair had never been cut, and it was done up in seven long locks. If they were ever cut off, he said, he would really become as weak as other men.

Feeling sure that he had told her the truth at last, Delilah planned to cut off his hair that very night, and she invited the lords of the Philistines to come up and see the result.

After Samson had fallen asleep, she had a man shave his head. The seven beautiful locks, the symbol of his devotion to God, fell to the floor, and his strength went with them.

"Samson, the Philistines are upon you!" she cried, but he couldn't do a thing about it. He tried to put up a fight, but "the Lord had left him."

Now he was made a prisoner. The Philistines put out his eyes, bound him with chains of bronze, and set him to work in a treadmill.

Poor Samson! What a miserable failure he had made of everything! It is hard to think that the blind, fettered man in the treadmill was once that little boy his parents had loved so dearly, the boy God had counted on to deliver Israel. How old Manoah and his wife must have wept over him and wished that somehow they might have stopped him from going with those heathen girls! But it was too late now.

As that treadmill went round and round and round, Samson had time to think of all his mistakes and the life he might have lived. In shame and sorrow he turned back to God and pleaded for one more chance.

As week after week and month after month went by, he noticed that his hair was growing again. And every inch it grew seemed to bring him closer to God. Gradually he felt his old strength coming back.

Then one day he was let out of the treadmill. He heard people talking about a great feast to Dagon, god of the Philistines. Someone told him that he had been released so he could entertain the merrymakers.

He guessed where he was being taken. He had been to the place before and remembered that there were two big pillars in the center of the building that supported the roof. An idea came to him. He asked the lad who was leading him by the hand to show him where the pillars were, so he could lean on them.

When the boy brought him to the place, he cried from the depths of his soul, "O Sovereign Lord, remember me. O God, please strengthen me just once more, and let me with one blow get revenge on the Philistines for my two eyes. Then Samson reached toward the two central pillars. . . . Bracing himself against them, his right hand on the one and his left hand on the other, Samson said, 'Let me die with the Philistines.' Then he pushed with all his might."

Suddenly there was an awful rending noise as the pillars toppled and fell. The whole place came crashing down upon him, together with 3,000 people who had been sitting on the roof. "Thus he killed many more when he died than while he lived."

And so Samson died, the strongest man who ever lived. If he had just tried to please God instead of himself, he might have been one of the greatest men in history. ✑

Gleaner Girl

(Ruth 1-4)

OUT OF all the darkness and sadness of the days when Israel was ruled by the judges comes one of the sweetest stories ever told. It is about a girl called Ruth, who belonged to the Moabites, long-time enemies of Israel.

As a child, I suppose she heard only bad things about the Israelites, and if she hadn't met Naomi, maybe she never would have known any better. Naomi was the mother of two boys about Ruth's age. One was called Mahlon, the other, Kilion. Their father's name was Elimelech and the four of them had come all the way from Bethlehem to Moab because of a famine in their own country.

After Elimelech's death Ruth and Mahlon fell in love and married. Also a girl friend of Ruth's named Orpah, married Kilion. The five of them were very happy together, for Naomi was the nicest mother-in-law any girl could wish to have. She loved her daughters-in-law dearly, and they loved her just as much.

137

Naomi was a godly woman, and she must have been very sorry when her sons married heathen girls. But she made up her mind to lead them, if she could, to love the God of Israel. She took every chance to talk to them of God's love and to tell them the stories she had heard from her parents long before.

Naomi explained to Ruth and Orpah how God created the world in the beginning and made it into a beautiful home for man, how Adam and Eve sinned and lost their garden home, and how God planned to give it back to them some day. She also told them about the Flood and the rescue of Noah and his family in the ark, of God's promises to Abraham, the dark days in Egypt, the great deliverance in the days of Moses, and all God had done for His people since then.

Ruth and Orpah loved to listen as Naomi talked to them. They especially liked to hear of the wonderful things she believed God would do for Israel in the future. Naomi may have told them that someday, through some sweet girl, Eve's Off-spring would come to crush the snake's head.

Ten years passed by. Then trouble came, and great sorrow. First Mahlon died, then Kilion, one after the other.

The sadness in that home must have been terrible. How Naomi, Ruth, and Orpah must have cried together. Poor things! It must have been hard for them to believe in the goodness of God. But they did.

Brave Naomi decided she would go back to her old home in Bethlehem, and the two girls said they would go with her. On the way, however, Naomi began to worry about them. She wondered whether she was doing right in taking them away from their own country. Perhaps they would be better off if they were to go back to their mothers.

"Go back, each of you, to your mother's home," she said to them kindly: "May the Lord show kindness to you, as you have shown to your dead and to me." Then she kissed them, and they all burst out crying again.

Both Ruth and Orpah said they would rather stay with her than go back to their homeland. They wouldn't leave her. They loved her too much. But Naomi said it was better for them to go back to their own homes. They must find new husbands, she said, and it would be easier to do this where they were known, among their own people.

They talked for a long time about it, and finally Orpah decided that maybe Naomi was right. She said goodbye with many tears and turned around to go back home. I can see her waving her last farewell before disappearing from view around a bend in the road.

But Ruth wouldn't go. In words that will live forever, she told Naomi, "Don't urge me to leave you. . . . Where you go I will go, and where you stay I will stay. Your people will be my

people and your God my God."

So Naomi and Ruth went on their way together, trudging slowly and sadly up the rough, steep mountain trail that led to Bethlehem. When they finally arrived at the village, everyone in town was excited. "Naomi is back!" the people cried, crowding around to hear the news she brought from the land of Moab.

"But where is your husband?" they asked. And, "Where are the boys?" Tearfully Naomi told her story. "I went away full, but the Lord has brought me back empty."

Fortunately the barley harvest was just beginning, so there was work to do and food to eat. Ruth offered to go into the fields and glean with the other village girls. In those days, grain was cut and gathered by hand, and what was left by the reapers could be picked up by the gleaners.

One day as she was busily at work, Boaz, the owner of the field, came by. Seeing a strange girl among his gleaners, he stopped to ask who she was.

The man in charge replied, "She is the Moabitess who came back from Moab with Naomi."

Boaz was interested. He had wanted to meet her, especially since Naomi was a relative of his. Calling Ruth to him, he told her he had heard about her kindness to Naomi and how she had willingly left her own country to come and live among strangers. "May the Lord repay you for what you have done. May you be richly rewarded by the Lord, the God of Israel, under whose wings you have come to take refuge," he said.

Smiling sweetly, Ruth thanked him for his kind words; and Boaz, liking her more every minute, told the reapers to let some of the sheaves drop where she could glean them. He wanted to make sure Ruth would have lots of grain to take home to Naomi.

As the days went by, Boaz and Ruth saw more and more of each other, and one day there was a wedding in Bethlehem. It must have been quite an event, for Boaz was very rich and Ruth was very poor, and a Moabitess too.

People must have talked about it for weeks, and they would have talked even more if they had known what this marriage would mean in the years ahead. For Ruth and Boaz had a son called Obed. And Obed had a son called Jesse. And Jesse had a son called David.

So Ruth—dear, kind, faithful Ruth—was the great-grandmother of King David. She was a direct ancestor of Joseph the husband of Mary who, more than 1,000 years later, in this very same village of Bethlehem, gave birth to the baby Jesus.

I am sure Ruth never dreamed that she would receive such a great honor when, far away in Moab, she listened to Naomi telling those wonderful stories of the God of Israel, the God of heaven and earth. How glad she will be, through all eternity, that she gave her heart to Him then. 🖋

PART FOUR

Stories of

Samuel *and* Saul

(1 Samuel 1:1-16:13)

Given to the Lord

(1 Samuel 1:1-2:11)

FOR MANY years the tabernacle built in the wilderness had been at Shiloh, about 25 miles (40 kilometers) north of Jerusalem. Joshua had set it up there after crossing the Jordan river. It looked pretty shabby by now, after being exposed to all kinds of weather for nearly 300 years. But it was still the center of worship for all who were faithful to the God of heaven.

The ark, the seven-branched lampstand, the altar of incense, and the table of the bread of the Presence, which young Bezalel had made with such wonderful skill, were still inside. Outside was the bronze altar, green with age, with smoke rising from a sacrifice just offered on it.

Eli was the high priest now. He was a very weak man, nothing like Aaron or Eleazar, who had held the office at first. His two spoiled boys, Hophni and Phinehas, were into all kinds of mischief. Because of their bad example, people visiting the tabernacle were beginning to lose all respect for the holy place. As you can imagine, God was very

← PAINTING BY CORRINE B. DILLON

Hannah had dedicated her son Samuel to the Lord before he was born, and now she brought him to live with the high priest Eli to be trained in the tabernacle for God's service.

displeased and began to look for another leader.

One day as Eli was sitting on a seat by one of the tent posts he noticed a woman who was acting strangely. She seemed to be making faces and talking to herself, and Eli thought she was drunk. Seeing a chance to do something to stop the wickedness going on around the tabernacle, he scolded the woman severely and told her to stop drinking.

"I'm not drunk," she said. "I'm just too sad to speak. I was only pouring out my heart to God."

Now Eli was sorry he had spoken so harshly, and he asked her what the trouble was.

Then Hannah told her story. She said she was married to a kind man called Elkanah, but she didn't have a baby. And oh, how she wanted a baby! Her friends had babies, lots of them, but she didn't have one. Not a single one. It didn't seem fair.

She had cried and cried about it until she couldn't cry anymore. Her husband had said to her, "Don't I mean more to you than ten sons?" but of course he didn't understand how she felt.

She had prayed again and again about it, but nothing had happened. Now she had come to the tabernacle once more to ask God to please give her a baby. If He did give her a child, she said eagerly, "I will give him to the Lord for all the days of his life."

Eli's heart was touched. "Go in peace," he said to her tenderly. "And God grant your prayer."

146

Hannah stopped sobbing. A beautiful smile spread over her tear-stained face.

From what Eli had said and the way he had said it, she felt sure her prayer would be answered. She went home happy for the first time in years.

God answered her prayer. In no time at all—or so it seemed to her—a lovely baby boy arrived, and she called him Samuel, which means "asked of God." So it was very fitting that Hannah should call her precious baby by that name.

How glad she was to have a little boy all her own! What made her happier still was the thought that this dear bundle of love had come to her straight from heaven in answer to her prayers.

The next time Elkanah went up to the tabernacle at Shiloh, Hannah stayed home so she could take care of her baby. Tenderly she watched over him, day after day and month after month. She treasured every precious minute she had him with her, for she had not forgotten her promise to give him to the Lord.

When at last Samuel was big enough to feed himself and run around on his own, she took him to Eli.

At first the old man didn't seem to recognize her, so she

said, "As surely as you live, my lord, I am the woman who stood here beside you praying to the Lord."

Then she pointed to little Samuel, holding tightly to her dress. "I prayed for this child," she said. "So now I give him to the Lord. For his whole life he will be given over to the Lord."

Eli was astonished. He had never seen such earnestness, such devotion, such love for God, as he saw on Hannah's face at this moment. The happiness shining in her eyes was so different from the ugly, unkind looks he had seen so often on the faces of his sons. If only everyone in Israel would love God like this and be willing to give their children to Him, how different everything would be!

Reverently the old man bowed his head and worshiped. Hannah dropped to her knees and began to pray, "My heart rejoices in the Lord. . . . I delight in your deliverance. There is no one holy like the Lord; there is no one besides you; there is no Rock like our God."

This was no silent prayer, like the one she had prayed years before. She cried aloud for everyone to hear, "He raises the poor from the dust and lifts the needy from the ash heap; he seats them with princes and has them inherit a throne of honor."

Hannah felt like a princess herself at that moment. And she knew in her heart that Samuel, her precious little Samuel, was now a prince of God. She had given him to the Lord of glory for the rest of his life—and even longer than that—forever and ever!

148

Voice in the Night

(1 Samuel 2:18-21; 3:1-21)

I WOULDN'T be surprised if Samuel cried himself to sleep that first night he was left alone with Eli. He was only a little boy, and he had never been away from his mother before.

As for Hannah, I am sure she cried all the way home as she thought of her lonely darling in the old tabernacle. She was even more worried when she thought of what those two big bullies, Hophni and Phinehas, might do to him. Yet in her heart she was sure that she had done right. After all, Samuel had come to her as a special gift from God, and she had promised to give him to the Lord.

Day after day Hannah thought about her precious boy and prayed for him. Whenever she could find time, she worked on a little coat for him. She wanted to take it with her to Shiloh the next time she went with her husband to offer the yearly sacrifice.

What a meeting that was! Can't you see little Samuel running to her with outstretched arms, crying, "Mamma!

149

Mamma! O Mamma dear! You have come to see me at last!"

She never forgot her dear boy for a moment, even though God eventually gave her three more sons and two daughters. Year after year Hannah came to Shiloh, bringing a new coat with her each time. And each one was a little longer and a little wider, as one birthday followed another, and he grew bigger and bigger.

During all these years, Samuel kept himself busy around the tabernacle, doing all sorts of things to help Eli. There must have been a great deal of cleaning and polishing and clearing up that needed to be done, all jobs that a boy his age could do so well.

Eli grew to love him dearly. He must have told Samuel the whole wonderful story of how God had given the tabernacle services to His people. He must have explained how the services taught the people about God's own great sacrifice to save them from sin, and how they helped prepare the people for the day when they could live in the Garden of Eden again.

150

VOICE IN THE NIGHT

Samuel loved to listen to the old man's stories of long ago, and he learned a great deal about God's dealings with His people.

Then one night something very wonderful happened. Samuel had finished his work for the day, and had gone to his bed. Everything was quiet in the tabernacle, and the flickering lamp was casting strange shadows on the walls and ceiling. Suddenly he heard someone call his name.

"Samuel."

Thinking that Eli must want something, he jumped up and ran to the old man. "Here I am," he said.

"I didn't call you, " said Eli. "Go and lie down again."

A little while later the voice called again. "Samuel."

Obediently Samuel got up again and ran to Eli. "Here I am," he said. "You *did* call me."

"No, my son," said Eli. "I didn't call you. Lie down again."

Puzzled, Samuel went back to his bed. Somebody had called him, he was sure. If it wasn't Eli, who could it be? No one else was around, as far as he knew. Then he heard the voice again.

"Samuel."

Once more he ran to Eli. "You did call me," he said.

Eli was puzzled now. Clearly someone had spoken to the boy. He guessed it must be God. Gently

he said to Samuel, "Go, lie down, and if you hear the voice again, say, 'Speak, Lord, for your servant is listening.' "

Very excited now, Samuel hurried back to bed. But not to sleep. How could he? Instead, he lay there wide awake, listening. Would the voice speak again? And would it really be God?

Then he heard it—gentle, kind, and tender—just the way God would speak to a young boy. "Samuel, Samuel."

Trembling, Samuel whispered, "Speak, for your servant is listening."

Then God told him of the trouble that was about to come to Eli because he had not trained his boys to do right and had let them do so many wicked things around the tabernacle.

Samuel didn't sleep the rest of that night. He just lay there tossing and turning until morning, wondering whether he should tell Eli what God had said to him. He loved his old master dearly, and didn't want to hurt him. But, oh dear, what was he supposed to do with such a message?

Eli settled the matter for him in the morning. He hadn't slept much that night either. Naturally he wondered why God had chosen to speak to one as young as Samuel instead of to him, the high priest. And he was filled with curiosity to know what God had said.

"Samuel, my son," he said, as he heard the boy up and about again in the morning. "What did God say to you? Don't hide it from me."

Slowly, sadly, Samuel began to speak. Little by little he

153

← PAINTING BY CORRINE B. DILLON

When Samuel heard a gentle voice calling him in the middle of the night, he remembered what Eli the priest had told him and cried out eagerly, "Speak; for thy servant heareth."

told the whole story, "hiding nothing." When he was finished Eli said, "He is the Lord; let him do what is good in his eyes."

Nothing more happened that day or the next. But as Samuel went about his tasks he couldn't help thinking about that voice in the night. It was such a sweet and kindly voice, something like his mother's, which he heard so seldom now. Perhaps he would hear it again. He hoped so.

He often listened for God's voice before he went to sleep. Then he began to talk to God and wait for His answers.

How very wonderful! A little boy talking with the great God of heaven! Soon they were good friends.

"The Lord was with Samuel as he grew up," the Bible says. "The Lord continued to appear at Shiloh, and there he revealed himself to Samuel through his word."

Dangerous Plunder

(1 Samuel 4:1-6:16)

YEARS went by. Samuel grew to manhood and became known through all Israel as a prophet of God. How proud his mother must have been of him—and how glad that she had given him to the Lord when he was a little boy!

So far the message he had passed on to Eli from the Lord had not come true. Eli was still alive. His two sons, Hophni and Phinehas, were behaving worse than ever. But Samuel knew it could not be long before something would happen to cause God's word to be fulfilled.

One day messengers arrived at Shiloh from the camp of Israel to say they wanted to take away the ark. The army had been defeated in battle with the Philistines, and the leaders had decided that their only hope of victory was to have the sacred ark with them.

Eli did not like to see the ark taken from the Most Holy Place. But Hophni and Phinehas took no notice of anything he may have said. Together they carried the ark out

155

of the tabernacle to the camp.

"When the ark of the Lord's covenant came into the camp, all Israel raised such a great shout that the ground shook." The people believed the ark was some sort of magic charm that would bring them victory no matter what sort of lives they were living or how much evil was in their hearts.

How mistaken they were! The next day, as the Israelites went into battle again, they were slaughtered. Thirty thousand men were killed, including Hophni and Phinehas. "The ark of God was captured."

Meanwhile, up in Shiloh, Eli waited for news. He was deeply worried about his two sons and the ark.

As he sat on a seat near the tabernacle a man came hurrying up the mountain trail. His clothes were torn, and there was dirt on his head, a sign of mourning in those days. As he entered Shiloh and told his story, the people wailed aloud in sorrow.

"What is the meaning of this uproar?" called Eli, now 98 years old and blind. "What has gone wrong?"

Then the messenger came and told Eli all that had happened. "Israel fled before the Philistines," he said, "and the army has suffered heavy losses. Also your two sons, Hophni and Phinehas, are dead, and the ark of God has been captured."

As the man mentioned the ark of God Eli fainted. He fell backward off the seat, hit his head on the ground, and broke his neck.

At the same time, the wife of Phinehas also died as she gave birth to a little boy. With her last breath she called the baby "Ichabod, saying, 'The glory has departed from Israel'—

156

because of the capture of the ark of God."

Meanwhile, the Philistines carried the ark in triumph to the city of Ashdod and put it in the temple of their god Dagon. Of all the plunder they had taken from the Israelites that day, this was by far the most valuable. Not only was it covered with gold, it was, they thought, the secret of Israel's strength. But they soon found out that it was a very dangerous piece of booty.

They thought their victory proved that their famous idol was greater than the God of Israel, but the next morning they found Dagon lying face down on the ground before the ark. An angel must have pushed it over during the night.

The Philistines set Dagon up in his place again, but the next morning he was down on the floor once more, this time all broken to pieces. His head and his hands had been snapped off and left in the doorway, nearly frightening the priests out of their wits when they arrived to open the temple in the morning.

What could have happened to their god? they wondered. Who could have smashed him to bits like this?

They were still wondering when a large number of people in the town suddenly became very ill. So many died of a strange disease that the leading men of Ashdod got together and decided that they must get rid of the ark of God immediately. They felt sure it was the cause of all their trouble. So they sent the ark to the city of Gath.

As soon as the ark arrived in Gath, however, the same disease broke out there. More and more people became sick and died. So the people of Gath decided to send the ark to Ekron, and the same thing happened there.

After seven months of this the Philistines had had enough. Everywhere the people were saying to their leaders, "Send the ark of the God of Israel away; let it go back to its own place, or it will kill us."

At last the five rulers of the Philistines agreed to act. They called for the priests of Dagon and asked what they should do. These men advised that the ark be put on a new cart pulled by two cows, and taken to the road that led to the city of Beth Shemesh in the land of Israel.

If the cows left their calves behind, they said, and followed the road all the way to Beth Shemesh, then it would be clear that the Philistines had done the right thing and that all their trouble had come upon them because they had kept the ark.

Many people watched the cart as it left, and no one was sorry to see it go. You can imagine their thoughts as they saw the two cows, without any driver, go straight down the highway "lowing all the way; they did not turn to the right or to the left."

The five rulers of the Philistines were deeply interested in the progress of the cart. They followed right behind it, eager to see what would happen. And they could hardly believe their eyes as they saw those two cows pull the cart uphill, right into the land of Israel.

They must have said to each other, How wonderful is the power of the God of heaven.

An Unheeded Warning

(1 Samuel 7:5-8:22)

WHEN Hophni and Phinehas took the ark away from the Most Holy Place, they did more damage than they thought. That day the glory departed not only from Israel but from the tabernacle, too. The ark never came back to Shiloh.

With the ark gone and Eli dead, Samuel returned to his old home at Ramah, where his mother may still have been alive. She had given him to the Lord, and now he was back again, a strong, wise leader of His people.

Samuel built a house in Ramah and married. And from here he went out all over Israel, calling the people to turn from their sins and worship the God of heaven. "From year to year he went on a circuit from Bethel to Gilgal to Mizpah, judging Israel in those places."

During these years there was trouble between Israel and the Philistines. Samuel kept saying that if the people would just turn to the Lord with all their hearts, everything would be all right.

They would never need to be afraid of the Philistines again.

Once when he had called a meeting at Mizpah, word spread that the Philistines were on their way with a large army. Everybody was frightened, but Samuel went on with the service, praying to God for deliverance.

Suddenly there was a tremendous burst of thunder from the skies. The Philistines scattered, and the Israelites chased them clear to the border. Samuel set up a stone as a monument of the great deliverance and called it Ebenezer, saying, "Thus far has the LORD helped us."

Thanks to Samuel's able leadership, "the Philistines were subdued and did not invade Israelite territory again." The Israelites even recaptured such important cities as Ekron and Gath.

One day, when Samuel was getting old, the elders of Israel

came to Ramah to see him. They were worried about what would happen after his death. Sadly Samuel had not done any better than Eli in bringing up his sons. He had been so busy preaching and traveling that he hadn't taken time to train his boys, and now they were giving him a lot of trouble and disappointment. He had hoped that one of them, at least, could take his place when he died. But neither of them was good enough, and everybody knew it.

"You are old," said the elders, "and your sons do not walk in your ways; now appoint a king to lead us, such as all the other nations have."

Samuel was shocked. A king! Israel had never had any king but God. Hadn't God been far better than a king, since He had led them out of Egypt? Why should they want a king now?

Samuel was so upset that he left the elders and went away by himself to ask God what to do.

God told Samuel to do what the people wanted, and not to take their request as an insult to himself. "It is not you they have rejected," He said, "but they have rejected me as their king."

Samuel went back to the elders and warned them what would happen if they insisted on having a king. "He will take your sons," he said, "and make them serve with his chariots and horses. . . . Some he will assign to be commanders, . . . and still others to make weapons of war. . . . He will take your daughters to be perfumers and cooks and bakers. He will take

162

the best of your fields and vineyards and olive groves and give them to his attendants. . . . Your menservants and maidservants and the best of your cattle and donkeys he will take for his own use."

What he said was so true! But the elders would not listen to his warning. They got angry. "No!" they cried, "We want a king over us. Then we will be like all the other nations, with a king to lead us and to go out before us and fight our battles."

There was no way to change their minds. They were sure that a king was all they needed to get them out of their troubles. They were wrong, hopelessly wrong, but they couldn't see it. They had to learn by experience.

When Samuel told the Lord what the elders had said, God told him to do what they wanted. "Give them a king," He said.

So the elders went back to their homes, and Samuel began to search for a young man who might be worthy to be the first king of Israel.

Choosing a King

(1 Samuel 9:1-10:24)

WHAT would you do if you were asked to find someone to be a king? Where would you look for him? What kind of person would he be? This was Samuel's problem. The elders of Israel had said, "Give us a king." Now it was up to him to find one.

No doubt he thought of all the fine young men he had met on his travels through the country. There was that big, strapping fellow he had seen in a meeting at Gilgal, but no, he wasn't good enough. There was that nice-looking lad in a home he had visited at Bethel, but he wasn't strong enough. Somewhere there must be a young man who would be just right for the job, but who was he, and where could he find him?

Then one day God told Samuel that he wouldn't have to search anymore. The young man was on his way to him and would arrive in the city the next morning. "About this time tomorrow," God said, "I will send you a man from the land of Benjamin. Anoint him leader over my people Israel."

Early the next morning Samuel went to the city gate and

watched everyone who came in. As the people streamed by he wondered whether this man or that was the person God had chosen. Whoever it was, he would be the first king of Israel. But which one would it be?

Then "an impressive young man without equal" came into view. Tall, handsome, and powerfully built, he stood out among the crowd as if born to be a leader. He was one of the finest men Samuel had ever seen.

As this splendid youth, standing head and shoulders above everyone else, came toward Samuel, God said to the prophet, "This is the man . . . ; he will govern my people."

Of course the young man, whose name was Saul, didn't know anything about this. He had never seen Samuel before. For the past three days he had been searching for his father's lost donkeys, and all he could think about was where they could be. His servant had suggested that maybe the prophet who lived in this city would know where the animals could be found, and that's why he had come.

"Is the prophet here?" Saul asked.

"I'm the prophet," said Samuel. "And don't worry about the donkeys that were lost three days ago; they have been found."

How does he know about my father's donkeys? wondered Saul. How could he possibly have heard that they have been found? For, of course, there were no telephones in those days.

Then Samuel invited Saul and his servant to eat with him. When they walked into Samuel's house, about 30 people were already there. You can imagine Saul's surprise when he and his servant were given the most-honored seats. He was still more surprised when Samuel told his cook to bring the special portion of food he had reserved for this occasion and set it in front of Saul.

Everybody in the room must have wondered why the stranger was treated so well. Perhaps, some thought, it was because he had just come to town, or maybe he was related to Samuel in some way. Or perhaps, since he was such a big man, he needed extra food. But Samuel never said a word. He just let them think whatever they wanted to. Someday they would find out.

That evening Samuel and Saul had a long talk together under the stars on the flat roof of Samuel's house. Then they went to bed.

The next morning the prophet walked with Saul and his servant to the outskirts of the city to tell them goodbye. There he whispered to Saul, "Tell your servant to walk on ahead."

The servant obeyed. Then Samuel opened a small bottle of

oil he had brought with him and poured it on Saul's head. After that he kissed Saul, and told him he was now anointed to be leader of the Lord's people.

Something happened to Saul at that moment. As he turned to leave Samuel, "God changed Saul's heart." All his thoughts and plans were changed. Up to this moment he had been interested mostly in himself but now he began to think about others and what he must do for his people and his God.

Samuel told him that when he arrived at Rachel's tomb, he would meet two men who would tell him that his father's donkeys were found. Next, on the plain of Tabor, he would meet three men—one carrying three kids, one carrying three loaves of bread, and another carrying a bottle of wine. They would give him two loaves of bread. Then, when he got to a place called Gibeah of God, he would meet a company of prophets singing and prophesying and he would join them.

Everything happened exactly as Samuel had said, which helped Saul to believe that everything else the prophet had told him was equally true.

Some days later, Saul went to Mizpeh. Thousands of people were gathered there, and Saul guessed that this was the time when Samuel would present him as their king. He began to be afraid, and he hid among the baggage.

From where he was hiding, he could hear Samuel speaking to the people. Samuel reminded them of all God had done for Israel since He had brought them out of Egypt. Then he heard lots being cast to discover the tribe in which the new king would be found. *Perhaps the tribe of Judah would be chosen,* he thought, *or maybe the tribe of Simeon.* He hoped so, for that would mean he wouldn't have to be king after all.

But no. The tribe of Benjamin was chosen. His tribe. Then lots were cast among the families of Benjamin, then among

members of the family of Kish. Finally his name was called.

"Saul! Saul!" cried his friends. But he didn't answer. The great moment of his life had come, and he wasn't ready for it. Instead, he was hiding behind heaps of bedding, pots and pans, and bales of hay. And there at last his friends found him.

The excited people brought him to Samuel where he turned and faced the crowd. Samuel said, "Do you see the man the Lord has chosen? There is no one like him among all the people."

Saul would gladly have run away—back to his farm or anywhere—but he couldn't. Suddenly a great shout went up, "Long live the king! Long live the king!"

Saul Saves the People's Eyes

(1 Samuel 11:1-12:25)

NOT ALL the people of Israel were happy about the choice of Saul to be king. Some turned up their noses and said, "How can this fellow save us?"

Saul went back home and worked on his farm as usual. Here was one king who had no palace, no government, no army, and no police force. Many times he must have wondered what a king was supposed to do.

Then one day as he was driving a herd of cattle out of a field, news reached him that the Ammonites had surrounded Jabesh Gilead and threatened to put out the right eyes of all the people in the city.

Here was a challenge, and Saul rose to it. Now he knew what a king should do. Quickly he sent messengers throughout all Israel, calling for men to go with him to save the citizens of Jabesh Gilead from the cruel Ammonites. Three hundred and thirty thousand men came quickly, all ready for battle.

Saul's spirits rose at sight of this mighty army, and he told

170

the messengers from Jabesh Gilead to hurry home and say to their frightened friends, "By the time the sun is hot tomorrow, you will be delivered."

All that night the men of Israel marched, with Saul proudly leading them. Early in the morning they came upon the Ammonites and took them completely by surprise, defeating them so thoroughly that "no two of them were left together."

So Jabesh Gilead was delivered, and Saul saved the people's eyes. Everybody was so happy about this victory, the first under Saul's leadership, that some said, "Who was it that asked, 'Shall Saul reign over us?' Bring these men to us and we will put them to death."

"No, no," said Saul. "No one shall be put to death today, for this day the Lord has rescued Israel."

Samuel saw that this victory was a wonderful chance to

give Saul a better start as the new king. So he suggested that all the people make their way to Gilgal and "reaffirm the kingship." This they did. The tens of thousands who had answered Saul's call to save Jabesh Gilead moved on to Gilgal, flushed with the spirit of victory. There, though they had chosen him to be king before, they made him king again with great rejoicing.

Samuel offered sacrifices, and the people ate and drank to their heart's content. Things hadn't looked so good for a long time.

"Now here is the king you have chosen, the one you asked for," Samuel said to the vast assembly.

"If you fear the Lord and serve and obey him and do not

172

rebel against his commands, and if both you and the king who reigns over you follow the Lord your God—good! But if you do not obey the Lord, . . . his hand will be against you, as it was against your fathers."

Earnestly he pleaded with them, "do not turn away from the Lord, but serve the Lord with all your heart. . . . For the sake of his great name the Lord will not reject his people, because the Lord was pleased to make you his own. . . . But be sure to fear the Lord and serve him faithfully with all your heart; consider what great things he has done for you."

At that moment everybody wanted to do right and serve the Lord forever. But how quickly they forgot their good resolutions! How soon they were in trouble again!

173

The Price of Impatience

(1 Samuel 13:1-16)

SAUL had reigned less than two years when things began to go wrong again. He had kept 3,000 of the men who had answered his call to fight the Ammonites as a sort of bodyguard and sent the rest home. Of the 3,000 men who stayed, he gave 1,000 to his son Jonathan to lead.

Being young and headstrong, Jonathan stirred up trouble with the Philistines by attacking one of their garrisons. In revenge the Philistines gathered a huge army of 3,000 chariots and 6,000 horsemen, and "soldiers as numerous as the sand on the seashore," and marched against Israel.

When news of this new invasion reached the Israelites, they were scared to death. "They hid in caves and thickets, among the rocks, and in pits and cisterns." Many fled across the Jordan for safety. "Saul remained at Gilgal, and all the troops with him were quaking with fear."

Samuel had said he would meet Saul at Gilgal within a

week, but day after day went by, and he did not arrive. Meanwhile, more and more men ran away. By the seventh day, his bodyguard had dwindled to only 600.

The young king became very impatient. Why was Samuel waiting so long to come? Surely he knew how serious the situation had become. Soon there would be no army left at all.

Suddenly Saul made up his mind. He wouldn't wait for Samuel any longer. In Samuel's place he would offer the burnt offering. And why not? After all, wasn't he king?

So he killed the animal that was to be offered as a sacrifice and burned it on the altar. Hardly had the smoke blown away, however, when Samuel arrived. Saul hurried to greet him, but there was a grieved look on the old man's face.

"What have you done?" he said.

Saul did his best to explain. "When I saw that the men were scattering, and that you did not come at the set time, and that the Philistines were assembling at Micmash, . . . I felt compelled to offer the burnt offering."

"You acted foolishly," said Samuel sternly. "You have not kept the command the Lord your God gave you."

By failing to wait for Samuel and by offering a burnt

offering, which he was not supposed to do, Saul had revealed serious weaknesses in his character. He had shown that he wasn't the sort of man Samuel had thought he was. He wasn't wise enough or good enough to be a king, for he didn't know how to obey.

"But now your kingdom will not endure," warned the prophet. Then, as a parting thrust, he added, "The Lord has sought out a man after his own heart and appointed him leader of his people."

It was a hard thing to say at such a time, but no doubt Saul needed it. A moment later Samuel was gone, and Saul was left on his own—with only 600 men to face the advancing Philistines.

Looking at the dying embers of the sacrifice he had offered, he wished he hadn't been so rash. He wondered if God had really given up on him so soon.

Discouraged, he moved his faithful band of followers to as safe a place as possible in "the outskirts of Gibeah" and set up his headquarters under a pomegranate tree. Often he must have wished he had never gone looking for his father's donkeys. Then he would never have met Samuel and wouldn't have been made king. And he wouldn't have gotten into this dreadful difficulty.

He didn't know what to do next. Israel's cause looked hopeless. What could he do with just 600 men?

Brave Young Prince

(1 Samuel 14:1-45)

THERE was at least one person on Saul's side who was not discouraged, and that was Jonathan. He knew all about the 3,000 chariots and the 6,000 horsemen that the Philistines had, and how few men had stayed with his father. Yet he was sure God could still save Israel, if He wanted to.

One day without saying a word to his father, he slipped out of the camp with his armor-bearer and made his way through a rocky pass toward the army of the Philistines.

"Come," Jonathan said, "perhaps the Lord will act in our behalf. Nothing can hinder the Lord from saving, whether by many or by few."

That was a grand thing for him to say, and God loves young people with such faith and courage.

Together the two young men crept from boulder to boulder until they were almost within shouting distance of a Philistine outpost on the top of a steep cliff. As the armor-bearer was wondering what Jonathan would do next, the young prince whispered to him, "We will let them see us; and if they say, 'Wait till we come to you,' then we will not go up to them. But if they say, 'Come up to us,' then we will go up, and this will be a sign unto us that the Lord has delivered them into our hands."

So they stepped out from behind a boulder and shouted to the men above them.

"Look!" cried the Philistine soldiers with a sneer, "The Hebrews are crawling out of the holes they were hiding in." Since they could see only two young men in the valley, they said, "Come to us and we'll teach you a lesson."

This was the sign Jonathan had been waiting for. "Follow me," (TEV) he said to his armor-bearer as he started to climb toward the top of the cliff.

The Philistines were taken completely by surprise. They never expected the two young men to fight—not after climbing all the way up so steep a cliff. But they didn't know Jonathan or his armor-bearer.

Drawing their swords, the two young men struck down about 20 men. Suddenly, right in the middle of the fight, there was a great earthquake. The mountains seemed to tremble. Panic seized the Philistines. They began to fight one another.

By this time Saul's lookouts at Gibeah had noticed that something had gone wrong in the camp of the Philistines. The huge Philistine army seemed to be melting away.

Courage came back to the little band of 600 men. As quickly as they could, they ran toward the struggling mass of humanity, who were "striking each other with their swords."

More and more Israelites came out of their hiding places and joined in the battle. When the Philistines saw them coming, they started to run, and the Israelites won a very great victory. "So the Lord rescued Israel that day"—through the faith and bravery of Jonathan and his armor-bearer.

But Saul had done another foolish thing, which spoiled everything. For some unknown reason he had said to his soldiers as they went into battle, "Cursed be any man who eats food before evening comes." So, hungry as they were, the soldiers ate nothing all that day.

Some of them, as they pursued the Philistines, came to a forest and found a large honeycomb "on the ground," perhaps

179

in a hollow tree. How good it looked! But they didn't dare touch it, because Saul would put them to death.

At that moment Jonathan came on the scene and caught sight of the honey. Since he hadn't heard his father's order not to eat, he went right ahead and ate some of the honey.

"There'll be trouble about this," warned one of the men who saw him do it, but Jonathan laughed it off. He couldn't see why people shouldn't eat on a day like this. "Just see how much better I am for eating," he said, jokingly remarking that the victory might have been much bigger if everyone else had eaten some honey too!

Trouble came soon enough. Though nobody told Saul what Jonathan had done, he discovered that somebody had eaten food that day, and he swore that he would find out who it was.

He became angry that someone had disobeyed him, and quite forgot this was a day of triumph when everyone should be happy and thankful. He vowed that he would kill the culprit even if it were his own son.

He called all his men together and told them that they would be on one side, and he and Jonathan on the other side. Then he ordered lots to be cast between the two sides. This was done. And you can imagine his surprise when the lot fell upon himself and Jonathan. You could have heard a pin drop at that moment.

Then Saul ordered, "Cast the lot between me and

Jonathan my son." Again the lots were cast, and Jonathan was taken.

Now Saul was really in a difficult position.

"What have you done?" he asked sternly, while everyone looking on held his breath.

"I merely tasted a little honey," said Jonathan meekly. "And now must I die?"

His pride hurt, Saul said angrily, "May God deal with me, be it ever so severely, if you do not die, Jonathan."

Then a glorious thing happened. A roar of protest rose from the rest of the army. "No!" they cried. " 'Should Jonathan die—he who has brought about this great deliverance in Israel? Never! As surely as the Lord lives, not a hair of his head will fall to the ground, for he did this today with God's help.'

"So the men rescued Jonathan."

Obedience, Not Sacrifice

(1 Samuel 15:1-28)

NOT FAR from the land of Israel lived a people called the Amalekites. They had become so wicked that God said they must be destroyed. Much earlier He had sent fire from heaven to burn up Sodom and Gomorrah when they became too wicked. Now He sent Israel to wipe out the Amalekites. These people were so bad that there was no hope they would ever repent of their sins.

Samuel brought God's message to Saul and told him to "go, attack the Amalekites and totally destroy everything that belongs to them."

This was not to be an ordinary war but a divine punishment. No spoil of any kind was to be taken. Nothing was to be spared, not even the animals.

Saul understood perfectly well what he was to do. It wasn't a pleasant task, but since God had ordered him to do it, he made plans to carry it out. Once again he sent messengers through the land of Israel, calling men to join his army. Two hundred and ten thousand men answered his call this time.

The Amalekites didn't have a chance against so many. They were completely wiped out. Only Agag their king was taken alive—"and the best of the sheep and cattle, the fat calves and lambs."

All the worthless animals were destroyed, but those that looked strong and healthy—well, it seemed too bad to kill them too. After all, they were very valuable. Good animals were scarce.

So the 210,000 men marched back from Amalek, driving hundreds of sheep and cattle before them. They looked like an army bringing back the spoils of battle.

Saul was feeling very pleased with himself. His army had taken care of a nasty job, and the people were happy with the loot they had won. They had food for a long time to come. All in all, everything had turned out very well indeed. Surely Samuel would

be very glad and grateful when he heard the story.

But Samuel was neither glad nor grateful.

As the old prophet came into the camp, Saul, all smiles, hurried over to greet him. "The Lord bless you!" he said. "I have carried out the Lord's instructions."

"So!" said Samuel, looking at him sternly. "Then what is the meaning of the bleating of the sheep and the lowing of the cattle which I hear?"

"Oh, that," said Saul, ready with an excuse. "The soldiers brought them from the Amalekites; they spared the best of the sheep and cattle to sacrifice to the Lord your God, but we totally destroyed the rest."

"Stop!" cried Samuel. "Let me tell you what the Lord said to me last night."

"Tell me," said Saul.

"When you were little in your own sight," said Samuel,

"were you not made the head of the tribes of Israel, and the Lord anointed you king over Israel? And the Lord sent you on a mission and said, 'Go and utterly destroy the sinners the Amalekites.' Why then did you not obey the voice of the Lord, but pounced on the plunder and did evil in the sight of the Lord?"

" 'But I did obey the Lord,' Saul said. 'I went on the mission the Lord assigned me. . . . The soldiers took sheep and cattle from the plunder, the best of what was devoted to God, in order to sacrifice them to the Lord your God at Gilgal.'

"Does the Lord delight in burnt offerings and sacrifices," asked Samuel, "as much as in obeying the voice of the Lord? To obey is better than sacrifice, and to heed is better than the fat of rams."

Then he added these solemn words: "Because you have rejected the word of the Lord, he has rejected you as king."

Rejected! Saul was shocked. He had never thought that anything like that would happen. And all over a few sheep and oxen! Surely God would not take the kingdom away from him over a little point like that! But he had not learned how important obedience is in the sight of God.

"Forgive my sin," he cried, begging for another chance. But it was too late.

Samuel merely repeated what he had said before: "The Lord has rejected you as king over Israel!"

As the prophet turned to leave, Saul grabbed his garment,

trying to hold him back, and the garment tore.

Looking at the tear, Samuel said, "The Lord has torn the kingdom of Israel from you this day and has given it to one of your neighbors, to one better than you."

So there was no hope. None. Saul was heartbroken. How foolish he had been! What a price he had to pay for his mistake!

That night he lay in his tent, listening to the bleating of the sheep and the lowing of the cattle he should have destroyed. Over and over again, he must have repeated to himself those striking words Samuel had said to him, "To obey is better than sacrifice, and to heed is better than the fat of rams."

To obey . . . to obey . . . to obey.

So he learned, too late, that obedience, not sacrifice, is what God wants most from us.

God Finds Another Boy

(1 Samuel 16:1-13)

SAUL lay in his tent that night, thinking about everything Samuel had told him. He began to wonder what the prophet could have meant when he said that the kingdom would be taken from him and given to a neighbor of his, someone who was better than he.

A neighbor! he thought. Which neighbor?

His mind ran over all the people he knew—the man who ran the farm next to his, or one of the more capable men in his army, or Jonathan. Yes, what about Jonathan? Was he going to be punished because of his father's sin?

However hard he tried, Saul could find no answer to his questions. If God was looking for another king, He hadn't given a hint as to who it might be. That is, not to Saul.

But He had to Samuel.

"Fill your horn with oil. . . . I am sending you to Jesse of Bethlehem," God had said to him. "I have chosen one of his sons to be king."

When Samuel arrived at Jesse's home, he soon discovered

187

that he had a bigger problem than he had expected. For Jesse had many sons, all of them tall, strong, handsome young fellows. How was he to tell which one God had in mind to be the next king of Israel?

Of course Samuel didn't tell anybody why he had come. That wouldn't have been wise. Instead he said he had come to offer a sacrifice, and everybody in town believed that was the only reason he was there.

After the sacrifice, Samuel asked Jesse to introduce his sons to him, and he was very happy to do so.

First was Eliab, the eldest. He was so tall and good-looking that Samuel felt sure this was the lad he was to anoint. But as he was reaching for his horn of oil, God told him not to look at the young man's face or height, "for I have rejected him. The Lord

does not look at the things man looks at. Man looks at the outward appearance, but the Lord looks at the heart."

Just why God refused to take Eliab, the Bible does not say. There must have been some weakness in his character that made him unfit to be a king. His father and mother didn't know about it, and neither did his brothers or friends. But God knew, and that was enough.

Then Jesse called his second son, Abinadab. But as Samuel greeted him warmly, God whispered that He hadn't chosen this lad either.

Next came Shammah, and the same thing happened again.

Jesse brought his fourth son, his fifth, his sixth, and his seventh. But as the boys were introduced, God kept saying to

Samuel, "Not this one," "Not this one," "Not this one."

By this time Samuel was really puzzled. God had refused all seven of Jesse's sons, and, so far as he could see, there were no more. What could be the matter? Had he made a mistake? Should he look them all over again?

Then he got a bright idea. "Jesse," he said, "are these all your sons?"

"Well, no," said Jesse. "There is still the youngest. He is out caring for the sheep."

"Send for him," said Samuel, all excited now. Surely, he thought, this must be the boy God had in mind. Eagerly he waited for him to come.

Meanwhile, out on the rolling hills, young David lay on his back looking up at the white fleecy clouds chasing each other across a bright blue sky. As he hummed softly to himself his father's sheep quietly nibbled the short grass all around him. Their gentle bleating added to the peacefulness of the scene.

Suddenly the stillness was broken by a distant shout.

"David! David!"

David jumped to his feet. Someone was calling his name. It was one of his father's trusted servants.

"I'm over here. What do you want?" David called back.

The servant came running up the hill, panting.

"What's the matter?" asked David.

"Your father wants you at once. Samuel is here."

"Samuel? Not the prophet Samuel?"

"Yes. He is staying for dinner, and he wants to see you."

"To see me? Oh no! Why would he want to see me?"

191

← PAINTING BY HARRY ANDERSON

As soon as the prophet Samuel saw David's smile and the goodness that shone out of his beautiful eyes, he knew that this was the boy God had chosen to be anointed king of Israel.

"But he does, and your father says you are to come right away."

Just what David did with the sheep we are not told. Perhaps the servant stayed to care for them. Anyway, like the obedient boy he was, he ran home as fast as he could, wondering what in the world was happening and why the great prophet Samuel, of all people, wanted to see him.

There was no time to clean up. Jesse hurried him right into the presence of Samuel.

Scared at having to meet such a famous man, David blushed all over. But his kindly smile, his friendly bearing, and the goodness that shone out of his beautiful eyes won Samuel's heart at once. At the same instant the prophet heard God say, "Rise and anoint him; he is the one."

Without a word, Samuel took his horn of oil and poured it on David's head.

From that moment everything was different. Though Samuel had said nothing about what God was planning for David, Jesse and his wife were sure that some great destiny lay ahead of their youngest son. The seven older boys must have had the same idea about their little brother. As for David, though he went back to caring for his father's sheep, "from that day on the Spirit of the Lord came upon David in power."

God had found another boy. Someday, if he was good enough, wise enough, true enough, he would be king of Israel.